Warwickshire County Council

Ken ''/14			K

This item is to be returned or renewed before the latest date above. It may be borrowed for a further period if not in demand. **To renew your books:**

- Phone the 24/7 Renewal Line 01926 499273 or
- Visit www.warwickshire.gov.uk/libraries

Discover • Imagine • Learn • *with libraries*

Warwickshire
County Council

Working for
Warwickshire

CHARCUTERIE

CHARCUTERIE

how to enjoy, serve and cook with cured meats

rps

RYLAND PETERS & SMALL
LONDON • NEW YORK

Miranda Ballard

photography by Steve Painter

To Anne, for the wins.

DESIGN, PROP STYLING AND PHOTOGRAPHY Steve Painter
EDITOR Kate Eddison
PRODUCTION David Hearn
ART DIRECTOR Leslie Harrington
EDITORIAL DIRECTOR Julia Charles
PUBLISHER Cindy Richards

FOOD STYLIST Lucy McKelvie
INDEXER Diana LeCore

First published in 2014 by
Ryland Peters & Small
20–21 Jockey's Fields
London WC1R 4BW
and
519 Broadway, 5th Floor
New York, NY 10012

www.rylandpeters.com

10 9 8 7 6 5 4 3 2 1

Text © Miranda Ballard 2014
Design and photographs ©
Ryland Peters & Small 2014

Printed in China

ISBN: 978-1-84975-567-2

A CIP record for this book is available from the British Library. US Library of Congress CIP data has been applied for.

NOTES

- All spoon measurements are level unless otherwise specified.
- All eggs are medium (UK) or large (US), unless otherwise specified. Uncooked or partially cooked eggs should not be served to the very old, frail, young children, pregnant women or those with compromised immune systems.
- Fruit and vegetables are medium-sized, unless otherwise stated.
- Chillies are fresh, unless otherwise stated.
- When a recipe calls for the grated zest of citrus fruit, buy unwaxed fruit and wash well before using. If you can only find treated fruit, scrub well in warm soapy water before using.
- Ovens should be preheated to the specified temperatures. We recommend using an oven thermometer. If using a fan-assisted oven, adjust temperatures according to the manufacturer's instructions.
- To sterilize preserving jars, wash them in hot, soapy water and rinse in boiling water. Place in a large saucepan and cover with hot water. With the saucepan lid on, bring the water to a boil and continue boiling for 15 minutes. Turn off the heat and leave the jars in the hot water until just before they are to be filled. Invert the jars onto a clean dish towel to dry. Sterilize the lids for 5 minutes, by boiling or according to the manufacturer's instructions. Jars should be filled and sealed while they are still hot.

FOOD SAFETY

- The information in this book is based on the author's experience. Guidelines for safety are included within recipes, and these should be followed. Neither the author nor the publisher can be held responsible for any harm or injury that arises from the application of ideas in this book.
- Use the freshest meats possible for home-curing. Ensure all tools and working surfaces are clean. Store all meats in a refrigerator.
- Uncooked or partially cooked meats should not be served to the very old, frail, young children, pregnant women or those with compromised immune systems.

MIRANDA BALLARD and her husband Roland left behind their media careers to start their own food company, Muddy Boots, in 2008. Their gourmet meat products are now available throughout the UK. They have now opened their first store, The Modern Meat Shop, in London, where they sell premium meat and charcuterie in a modern, friendly and welcoming environment.

STEVE PAINTER worked for Ryland, Peters & Small for more than 10 years, designing and art directing books. He now lives in the British seaside town of Hastings, where he shot, styled and designed this book.

CONTENTS

INTRODUCTION

Will you allow me to start with an assumption? If you bought this book, or someone thought this book might be a good gift for you, then I think we already agree about how to source our meat. I think that we're the ones upholding our side of the deal, the deal between humans and livestock. That, as the term 'animal husbandry' reminds us, we are part of a binding contract that relies on our respect for animals and their welfare.

I think we're the ones who appreciate that there are challenges involved in finding where this contract is commercially viable, but we have taken the time to learn where that balance lies. We're proud to understand the difference between 'clean' meat and cheap meat.

I think you'll already anticipate that whenever I refer to 'farming', I mean 'good farming', when I talk about 'meat', I mean 'good meat', and when I cover the wonderful range of products under the heading of 'charcuterie and salumi', it's understood that the entire process of the procurement and production of these products should uphold the contract between humans and livestock.

So I'm not going to talk about how to find and afford these products, because I know you're already with me on this. I'm sure that you share the same enjoyment and confidence from making a recipe with good meat and knowing that it will deliver on taste.

I'll just carry on then – and I really hope you enjoy the ideas and recipes in this book!

Three reasons why I love charcuterie.

The first reason is that it's a gift to home cooking – it's a gift of expertise, passion and time. These products can sometimes take longer to produce than the time it takes to build a skyscraper (Jamón Ibérico springs to mind – see page 20). When you think about the processes involved, you realise how much effort goes into the products that you can buy pretty conveniently and affordably nowadays. The process starts in

the same way as it does for raw meat. Let's take a quick look at cured pork products like salami and chorizo, for example:

The farmer plans for the boar and sow to mate, then the sow gives birth to piglets. The piglets are weaned, then the grown pig is sent to slaughter. The carcass is butchered, then the pork is sold to the customer. Now, with cured meat products, just before the pork is sold to the customer, an expert steps in and says, 'Hang on. Lend it to me for a bit and I'll use all my skills, resources and experience to make it into another product... then you can buy it'. It's like having a top chef step in and prepare your pork shoulder or your sirloin steak for you so that you can eat it immediately or just pop it in a recipe; they add taste and value to a product before it even reaches you.

The second reason is that I find it really tasty. Homo sapiens evolved to farm animals because we realized that, with limited food resources around us at the time, we could flee and/or fight for a lot longer if we'd eaten fats, protein, iron and vitamin B that day, as opposed to just leaves and berries. The strength we got from this diet became affiliated with our tastebuds and food preferences, and we went searching for what is basically fuel. I realise it's a different world we live in today, and a sensible and educated approach to vegetarianism and even veganism is entirely possible, because we have an unlimited resource of food products, knowledge, supplements and food science to be able to compensate for the strength and energy that meat once gave us. However, it doesn't mean that the combination

of salt, meat and fat doesn't still taste terrific to the tastebuds I inherited from my cavewoman ancestors millions of years ago.

The third reason, funnily enough, comes from the very reason cured meat developed in the first place – out of necessity in man's battle against bacteria. Yes, I'm talking shelf-life, still the biggest commercial challenge in the food industry today and the ticking clock that keeps us and our little meat business awake at night. Curing and fermentation developed simultaneously around the globe in almost every culture and race (in many different forms) because we needed to find ways to preserve our food. We're spoilt for choice nowadays with technology in the home, but there's still a simple challenge when you buy some fresh meat on a Monday and your plans change during the week, so you still haven't eaten it by Friday. Given that it

already took three days at the start of the logistics chain to get the meat from the abattoir to the supermarket or butcher's shop before it reached you... well, you're out of shelf-life. The really practical and wonderful joy of something like a stick of chorizo in your refrigerator, is that it lasts a long time. When you open your refrigerator and wonder what on earth you're going to have for supper that night (because you know you haven't been shopping for a bit!), you can whip up a bowl of pasta with some sautéed shallots and diced chorizo, or make a quick tart with saucisson sec, or a nutritious fritatta with pancetta. Freezing is wonderful and helpful, but it's even easier to have some cured meat in the refrigerator that doesn't need defrosting. I think the really significant rise in its popularity in the last 10 years, outside of the Mediterranean countries where it has existed for centuries, is because we're all trying to waste less food; cured meat almost never gets thrown away.

Those are my three main reasons for loving charcuterie as I do, and it's the first reason that ensured this collection of recipes was such a pleasure to put together... a pleasure and also a total dream because, well, what a fraud am I?! Months of care has been taken by somebody who cured the product, and I just swing in on the home stretch and form a recipe around it or pair it with accompaniments... and then I'm trying to take the credit. However, I'm not sorry, and I urge you to be the same, because I intend this collection to be a celebration of charcuterie and salumi and I have total admiration for the work done at the source of the meat curing. It's thanks to the dedicated work of these producers that we can have confidence in knowing that we're starting a recipe with an ingredient that is already excellent and will definitely deliver in terms of taste.

In chapter five, there are some ways to try curing meat simply in your own home, so you too can have a little glimpse into the science and care behind the process.

CHARCUTERIE AND SALUMI

By way of an introduction to charcuterie and salumi, here are answers to some of the most commonly asked questions.

To what do the terms refer exactly?

The term 'salumi' isn't a spelling mistake, it covers all cured meat products, including salami. It comes from the Latin term 'salume', meaning 'salted meat'.

'Charcuterie' is used more specifically for pork products, which make up the vast majority of the most popular cured meat products. The French have a 'boucher' for beef, lamb and poultry, etc and then a separate 'charcutier' for pig products because they have so many. The 'charcuterie' is the shop where this pork range is sold, so it's also now used as a term to cover a huge range of pork products from fresh and cured sausages to pâtés, roast ham joints and bacon.

This collection of recipes contains far more pork products than any other meats, but this is based on the ratio of what is sold (and therefore produced), and pig is just the cured-meat winner!

What's the difference between ham, bacon, gammon and pork?

Basically, fresh meat from a pig is pork. Then when it's cured it becomes ham, gammon or bacon. Ham is cured meat from the hind leg – either boned or with the leg bone still in it, as you sometimes see hanging in the windows of tapas restaurants or charcuteries. Technically, it's only 'ham' if it's been cured separately from the rest of the body. If the body has been hung and cured in one piece, the joint is 'gammon'. It's only 'gammon' while it's raw and it's generally called 'ham' once it's cooked, even if it wasn't cured as a separate joint. Got it? Oh yes, and 'bacon' refers to the cured pork from the belly ('streaky/fatty bacon') and loin (loin being the sides, above the belly, which is the most common

bacon – showing the large oval meat shape above the smaller streaky section, and a line of fat down one side).

Minced/ground pork products like fresh and cured sausages (such as salami and chorizo) use meat from the neck and shoulder of the pig.

Why does cured meat keep so much longer?

This is the fascinating part. How come you can keep some cured meat products for up to a year but even a sealed and treated pack of minced/ground pork only keeps for 9 days?

Salt is the answer. Long before there were refrigerators, Europeans were using salt to preserve their food. So much so, the word 'salary' comes from the Latin for salt, because it was so valuable for preserving food that people were paid in quantities of salt.

In simple terms, the process involves 'sucking' all the bacteria out and then 'sealing' it to stop any bacteria coming back. You know how a can of beans keeps a long time? Well, that's because the beans get heated so that all the bacteria are killed, and then they are sealed in a can so that no new bacteria are able to get in there. The same concept is used for curing meat ... the salt sucks out all the moisture and, with it, the bacteria. Then the salt also alters the acidity level of the meat so that it becomes like a bacteria antidote and prevents any new bacteria forming. Like the defences of the baked bean can, the cured meat doesn't let any new bacteria get into it again.

When doing this process at home, great care must be taken, as bacteria can be very dangerous, if they do get into the meat. Trust your instincts – discard any meat that is mouldy or smells unpleasant or 'off'.

What do the different curing terms mean?

They are different methods of getting the salt in and around the meat so that the bacteria is extracted, and can be simply explained as follows:

'Dry-curing' is covering the joint in salt.

'Wet-curing' is most commonly used for large-scale production of bacon and loin joints. The meat is soaked in, or injected with, brine (salty water).

'Air-drying' starts with dry-salting and then the meat is hung in temperature-controlled surroundings. As with hanging beef, this tenderizes the meat as well as ageing it to reach the acidity levels necessary to fend off bacteria.

'Smoking' has the same curing result but uses a different method. The smoke acts like a 'poison' for the bacteria, killing it off, rather than drawing it out. Smoked products generally derive from cooler Northern European countries, such as Germany, Poland and Britain, because it was a bit chilly to have meat hanging out in the barns.

'Comminuted' is a fancy word for minced-and-mixed-around-a-bit. Salami and chorizo, for example, use minced/ground pork from the neck and shoulder joints, which is combined with salts and seasoning, and then hung and air-dried.

Why does ham sometimes have a bone in it, and how can you buy a hind leg without a bone in it?

Since most of us don't own commercial-capacity refrigerators and ovens, buying a whole pig's leg with the bone in it isn't practical. Meat is muscle and there are three muscles on the hind leg. These can be removed whole from the bone and then 'tumbled', which, as the name suggests, means rolling them around in a big machine. During tumbling, proteins in the meat are released and become sticky, so when the three parts of meat are then put back together in a mould, they stay stuck together. That's why you'll get a white line of fat through the middle of a ham joint or in a slice of cooked ham, because that was actually the outside of one of the parts of the hind leg before it was tumbled.

Isn't it terribly fatty and bad for you?

Yes and no. Many cured meat products use pork that is 30% fat, but a lot of the curing processes reduce the saturated fats – if you gather the liquid that is drawn out on the first day of salting pork belly, for example, and let it set, you'll see how much the fat has been reduced. On top of that, you can always trim the fat down from the cured meat – just as you can with a bacon loin rasher/strip once it's cooked. Cured meat is also lovely and rich, so whereas you'd sit down to a 280-g/10-oz steak, you wouldn't eat the same weight of Parma ham – it's rarely sold in packs that weigh half that, unlike cheese, which is usually also at least 30% fat and is eaten in larger portions. Finally, it's up to you to reduce the fat content further if you like. You can grill/broil or bake salumi (see Salumi Chips, page 142), which will draw out more fat before eating it, or you can trim your meat. There are also lean options like cured beef (bresaola) and venison to choose from.

Of course salt intake has to be regulated too. However, although salt is absorbed by the meat, it is washed off after the initial salting. You'll see that the sodium level is around 1%, and there aren't any recipes in this book that suggest more than 100 g/3¾ oz. of salted meat per serving. Even my hungry carnivore of a husband doesn't look for more cured meat than that!

Why are there special names like 'Parma ham'? Isn't that the same as 'prosciutto'?

It basically is. There are many 'PDOs' or Protected Destinations of Origin in cured meat, to show where the product has come from and to ensure certain aspects of how it has been made. PDOs regulate products like Champagne, which has to come from select regions and adhere to certain practices to carry the name, otherwise it's just sparkling wine. Parma ham is such a product; its name ensures that it comes from a controlled area on the plains of the Po River in Italy. The name incorporates rules about which breeds of pigs can be used, when and how they're slaughtered, and the process of curing and ageing. Then a chap comes along with a pokey stick ('d'esto di cavallo') and tests every single cured joint to make sure it qualifies for the image of the crown on the packaging (and on the actual hind if you see a whole cured joint). The fact that so many of us refer to any type of prosciutto as 'Parma ham' is testament to a pretty impressive bit of brand-building! There are so many types of prosciutto to try, don't limit yourself to that from Parma, no matter how delicious.

What do I look for/ask for when I'm shopping?
I took a course with the Guild of Fine Foods in London, and there I learned a good test for texture. If you shut your eye and lightly press on your eyelid, that's the texture under your finger that you're looking for with cured meat. It needs to be soft and have some give. If you're buying a whole stick or joint of cured meat, it's likely you're spending a good bit of money, so don't be timid. Ask the person at the counter if you can have a latex glove or a bit of clingfilm/plastic wrap and if you can prod the outside; they should let you. If it's softer than your eyeball and really 'gives' it might be tainted or have been stored at too warm a temperature – not good. If it's really solid under your finger, it might be old or over-aged and it will be very chewy and hard – not good either. If you're buying it ready-sliced, the producer should have picked up on any problems before slicing and wrapping it so it's a safe-bet.

As I have said, good cured meat doesn't come cheaply – because of the cost of manufacture, care and skilled labour that goes into making it. That means you shouldn't be embarrassed to ask questions, nor to ask to taste a small piece if they're slicing it fresh for you. It won't cost the shop much at all to give you a little sample, and they should see that as a good investment. Of course, don't be cheeky and ask to try them all, at least not without buying something!

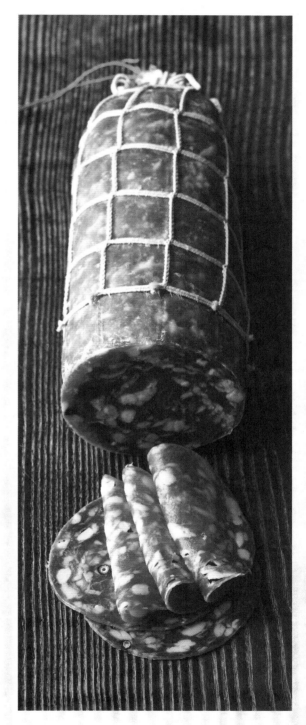

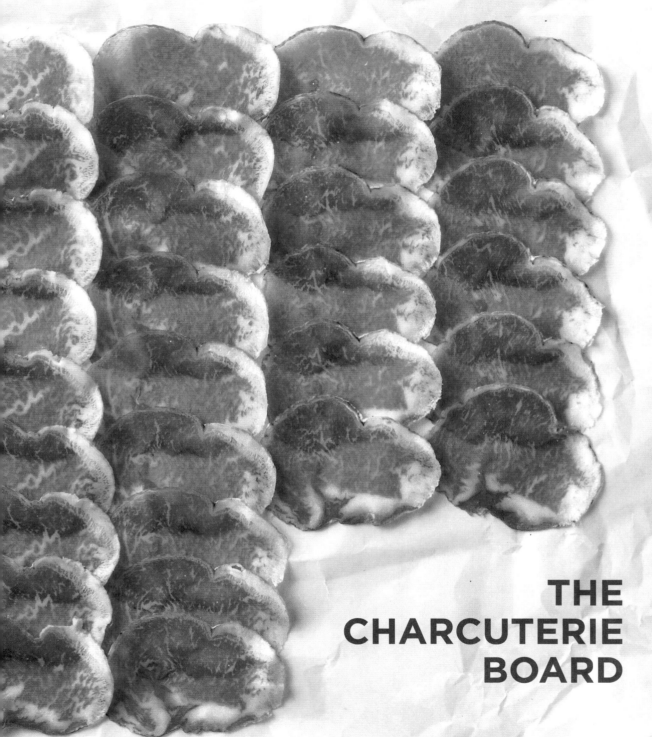

THE
CHARCUTERIE
BOARD

ITALIAN SALUMI BOARD

I'm an English red-head from the Worcestershire countryside but, for some reason, it's the Italian meats and accompaniments that really do it for me. I just love them, and when I was creating the recipes in this book, my tastebuds kept leading me towards traditional Italian products. Some of the best-known cured meat products available around the world are of Italian origin, so let's take a look at some of them.

Prosciutto crudo is perhaps the most common cured product where the meat isn't minced/ground, the most famous type being from Parma ('Parma ham' or prosciutto di Parma, pictured opposite). This is a whole hind leg of the pig, which is dry-cured in salt and then hung for up to a year (sometimes longer). The meat often comes from more mature pigs than for fresh pork products; fresh pork and sausages tend to come from pigs under 4 months old, whereas most forms of prosciutto require the animal to be at least 6 months old. **Coppa** or capocollo is a cured pork muscle that is sliced like prosciutto, but comes from the neck of the animal (pictured opposite).

Pancetta is more like bacon in style. It's wet- or dry-cured belly pork that is most commonly diced, fried and added to recipes. A home-cure recipe for pancetta is given on page 126.

Salami is probably the best known 'comminuted' (minced/ground) cured meat, and popular regional varieties include Milano and Napoli (pictured opposite). The process involves mincing/grinding the shoulder or neck muscle and combining it with seasoning and herbs, stuffing the mixture into a casing and air-drying it. **Mortadella** is 'the light pink' one but don't make the mistake of imagining it tastes anything like pork luncheon meat – the colour is comparable but that's it. The minced/ground pork is puréed so that it is very smooth. It is often mixed with pistachios as well as the seasoning and salts, and it's hung in a casing, like salami.

Bresaola is one of the best cured beefs from Italy and originates from the Lombardy region in the North. It is a dry-salted, lean cut of beef that is air-dried. **Pastrami** is usually made with brisket or topside. It is salted, spiced and dry-cured.

Suggested accompaniments
Bruschetta
Puttanesca Relish (see page 148)
Sun-dried or semi-dried tomatoes
Olives
Grissini
Crostini
Parmesan or pecorino cheese
Olive oil and balsamic vinegar

What to pair with your platter?
Having a glass of alcohol with your cured meat board isn't merely an indulgence. A good pairing can genuinely improve the flavour of each component by waking up the tastebuds and stimulating different parts of your tongue. One of the reasons we enjoy eating cured meat cold is that, unlike hot meat, it lasts a long time on our tongue – we don't just tenderize it with our teeth before swallowing it, it's too chewy to do that quickly, so we don't need to rush; why not have a sip of a drink in between to reset the tastebuds and build up to the next mouthful of cured meat.

Light and fruity wines are good with the bold flavours of Italian cured meats. You don't want to overpower the flavour of the ham. Good tipples to serve with any Italian selection are chilled Prosecco or crisp Pinot Grigio. Alternatively, go for a full-bodied Chianti or Montepulciano d'Abruzzo. You can also try a lightly chilled red wine, such as a Valpolicella. On a hot day, an ice-cold Italian beer, such as Peroni Nastro Azzurro, works well too.

FRENCH CHARCUTERIE BOARD

It is the French we have to thank for the word 'charcuterie', as pork products are so important to them that pigs get their own specialist butcher. A few years ago, I cycled through Western France, through some incredible wine regions. I ate Pain au Raisin until around 11 am, when I moved onto cheeses, and, after parking up my bicycle around 5 pm, would eat cured meats, rillettes and pâtés (and drink a lot of wine...). It was no surprise that although I cycled about 50 miles a day, I still managed to put on weight! But completely, utterly worth it, too. Here are some ideas for the perfect board.

There is a wide variety of hams (jambon) in France. Some are raw and air-cured (jambon cru), and others are smoked or cooked. Look for regional varieties marked Protected Geographical Indication (PGI), which ensures products are genuine.

The most ubiquitous PGI ham is **Jambon sec** – a dry-cured ham made from pigs that meet a minimum weight, and which has been dry-cured for at least 3 months (pictured opposite). Hams in this category include those produced in the Ardennes, Auvergne, Bayonne, Lacaune, Najac and Savoie regions. **Jambon sec superieur** is a variation that comes from pigs raised and butchered by traditional methods, such as Bigorre Ham from free-range Gascony black pigs raised in the Pyrénnées mountains. **Jambon de Bayonne** is a particular speciality of the Pays Basque region in southwest France and is prized for its rich, nutty flavour. It comes from pigs that enjoy a 'clean' diet, which includes chestnuts, acorns and beechnuts. The hind leg meat is salted (with local Salies-de-Béarn salt), then air-dried and matured for up to 10 months.

Jambon d'Ardennes is produced in northeastern France and has long been renowned the world over for its texture and very mild, slightly sweet flavour. This is not to be confused with **Ardenne Ham**, which is salted and air-dried for several months and has a fine, dry texture. This ham is produced in Belgium.

Saucisson sec is a dry-cured sausage (pictured opposite). Much like Italian Salami, it uses neck and shoulder muscle, minced/ground and comminuted with seasoning and spices, usually fresh garlic, black peppercorns and sea salt. It is hand-tied and cured for 30 days.

Pâté – the most famous pâté is fois gras, which is cooked and minced/ground fattened goose liver, seasoned, chilled and topped with melted butter (which seals the cooked meat underneath and extends the shelf-life). Concerns about animal-cruelty surround the controversial production of fois gras, so I would opt for a good chicken liver pâté, which makes an excellent alternative. Pâté is usually served as a spread to go on crisp Melba toasts, or try potted **rillettes.** These are similar to pâté but they are slow-cooked, are not puréed and don't traditionally contain liver. Their texture is rougher, more like shredded meat, and they are often spooned, rather than spread, onto a slice of crusty baguette. Try my recipe for Pork Rillettes on page 42. The technique and method can be used with other meats like beef and game. **Terrines** (or pâtés au terrine) are similar to pâtés but made with more coarsely chopped ingredients, baked in a loaf mould, sliced and served cold or at room temperature.

Suggested accompaniments:
Olive tapenade (see page 148)
Freshly sliced baguette
Cornichons
Cheeses such as Brie or Roquefort

What to pair with your platter:
A chilled glass of Sancerre or Champagne works well with French charcuterie, or try a punchy but dry rosé. A slightly chilled glass of red wine, such as a Pinot Noir, is also a good choice.

SPANISH BOARD

The consumption of chorizo in countries outside of Spain has increased hugely over the last few years. I once received an email from someone who had bought our beef meatballs with chorizo pieces mixed into them, and he finished his email with, "What did we do before chorizo?". This made me laugh and then actually have a think about the answer. As I mentioned in the introduction, we all take great pleasure in having a tasty, versatile meat product in our refrigerator that lasts a long time. Chorizo is an exciting option between cured meat and fresh sausages – it is endlessly versatile.

The best-known Spanish cured meat is, without doubt, **Chorizo**. This is made from minced/ground and seasoned pork, which gains its lovely smoky flavour from paprika and chilli/chili. The mix is stuffed into a casing and hung to air-dry. It can be eaten as it is and is also very adaptable for cooked recipes – perhaps more so than salami, because it contains slightly more oil.

Jamón Serrano (literally 'ham from the mountains') is whole cured ham, similar to prosciutto, and is usually served in thin slices. It has a lovely rich, dark flavour and comes from regions all over Spain.

Jamón Ibérico is a protected origin variety of Spanish cured ham (pictured opposite). Jamón Ibérico de Bellota is one of the most expensive meat products in the world. The pigs – usually Landrace breed – traditionally live to 2 years old and roam free in forests. For the last few months of their lives, they gorge happily on acorns, which adds around 20% more fat to them. The meat is so oily and fatty that when the hind leg is hung to air-dry, a little vessel is hung below to capture the oil that drips. It's rich, delicious and expensive. **Chorizo Ibérico de Bellota** is also popular and pricey; made from the comminuted shoulder and neck meat from those acorn-guzzling Iberian pigs (pictured opposite).

Cecina de León is a hind-leg of cured beef from the León region of Spain. The Spanish Cecina meat range occasionally uses horse- and goatmeat as well, however it is always produced by a dry salt-cure and hanging process. When sliced, it is a vibrant shade of maroon, with darker brown at the edges.

Spanish tapas is the tradition of serving little dishes of food with drinks. Traditional tapas include hams and chorizo, but they are also accompanied by some wonderful non-meat dishes. Originally, a tapa could have been as simple as a slice of ham or cheese that a drinker placed over his or her glass to stop flies going in. Today, tapas are just as important as the drink itself, and there is a huge variety of options, from hot to cold.

Suggested accompaniments:
Patatas Bravas
Olives
Marinated roasted red peppers
Rustic Spanish breads
Manchego cheese
Almonds

What to pair with your platter:
You could opt for a classic reds such as Rioja, Tempranillo or Garnacha, or really inspire that holiday mood with a refreshing, cold Spanish beer. A Spanish platter works very well with a fino sherry – it may not be the first thing you think of when selecting wines to serve with a platter of cured meats, but a dry sherry is a perfect pairing with Spanish meats. A dry rosé, such as one from the Navarra, would complement the rich flavours of the meats too. A chilled glass of Cava is a good choice with the strong paprika-based flavours of chorizo.

OTHER BOARDS

Using the word 'other' seems a bit mean here but, as I mentioned, I hope you'll forgive me for planning this collection to reflect the cured meat production around the world. If you specialize in producing and/or cooking with these meats, I salute you! As more and more people try them, they become more readily available in supermarkets. The Spanish and Italians talk about a sea breeze rolling over the hills, gathering the aroma from the arable farmland and flowing through the curing houses. The British, the Germans and the Poles might not be quite as poetic when it comes to the production of cured meats, but they definitely make ones that taste just as good, I reckon.

Germany is home to many flavourful cured meats. The most famous ham is **Black Forest Ham**, which is a dry-cured, smoked ham with a bold flavour. It is produced in the Black Forest region of Germany, and is one of the most popular hams eaten in Europe. Germany is also famous for its sausages, or **wurst**, which include the famous bratwurst, rohwurst and kochwurst. The Germans also make a vast selection of salami.

Some really interesting sausages come from Eastern Europe, and Poland in particular. **Kabanos** is a long-life smoky cured sausage made from pork. It is long and thin, and characteristically folded in half. **Wiejska** ('vee-esh-ka') is made from pork and veal, flavoured with marjoram and garlic. It is also folded into a 'U' shape. **Sapocka** ('sop-otz-ka') is lean pork loin which is cured, smoked and then roasted.

The United Kingdom has many traditional meats and sausages, even though the supermarkets today tend to stock more Italian and French products than traditional British meats. The most famous British sausage is **Black Pudding**, which is made from pig's blood, with oats and seasoning. It is particularly associated with a traditional English breakfast. **Haslet** is a meatloaf-style dish, made using offal/variety meats. **Haggis** is a classic Scottish sausage, made from sheep offal/variety meats with oats, onions and seasoning, traditionally encased in the animal's stomach. **Smoked Venison** (pictured opposite) is often minced/ground with a little fat from pork or beef, and smoked over English apple wood. Terrines are frequently seen in the UK, with **pheasant and other game terrines** being very popular when these meats are in season. Using game in a terrine is designed to add seasoning and tenderize the meat, as game meats can often be very lean.

Some general accompaniments:
Homebaked Oatcakes (see page 155)
Wholemeal Crispbread (see page 155)
Fig Chutney (see page 146)
Apple Slaw (see page 145)
Sauerkraut (see page 134)
Pickled onions
Smoked garlic

If it's too cold to dry-cure meats in Northern Europe, then it's definitely cold enough to get a little warmth from an accompanying drink:
German beers
Polish vodka
Polish nalewka (fruit- and spice-flavoured liquer)
English sparkling wine
English rosé wine
English sloe gin

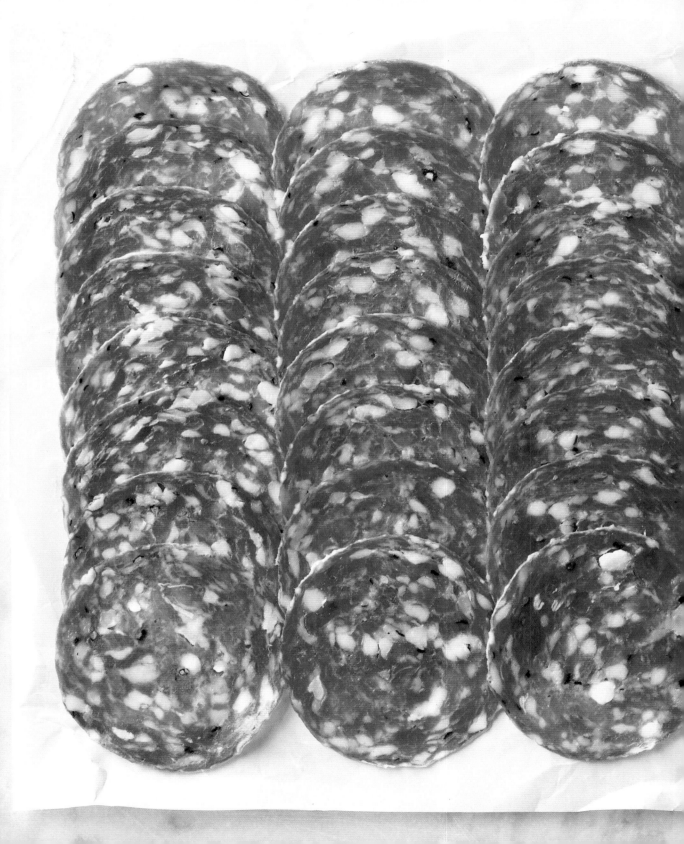

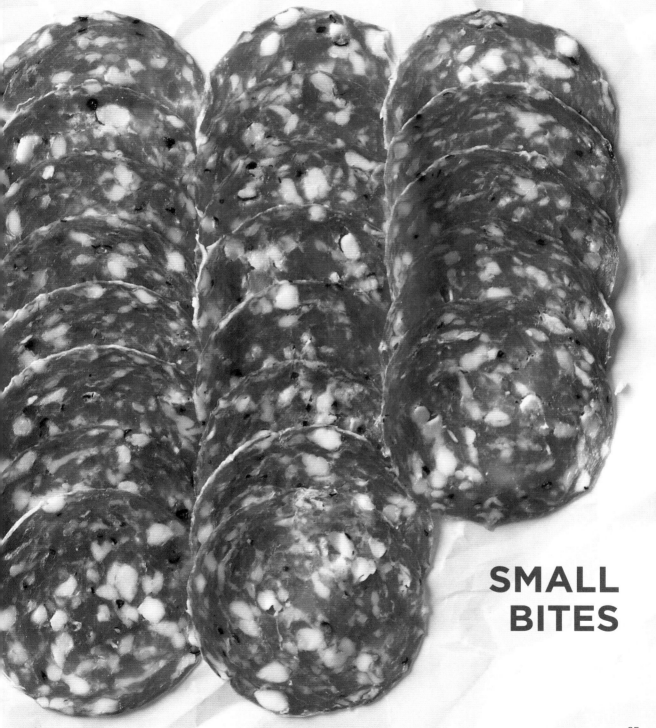

SMALL
BITES

CHORIZO AND SCALLOP SKEWERS

This is as lovely a combination of textures as it is of flavours. The scallops become slightly pink with the chorizo oil, and the taste of paprika permeates the soft flesh. I use these two ingredients together again in the Scallop, Chorizo, Chilli and Quinoa Stew (see page 109). I'm also a fan of frozen scallops. I find they cook beautifully and are great to have on stand-by. Given that chorizo has such a lovely long shelf-life, having a bag of frozen scallops means that this combination is on hand for all sorts of recipes – from canapés and stews to salads and risottos.

12 shelled scallops (or frozen scallops, defrosted)

12 x 1-cm/½-inch cubes chorizo

sea salt and freshly ground black or pink pepper

olive oil, for frying

paprika, for sprinkling

MAKES 12

First fry the scallops in a little olive oil in a frying pan/skillet over high heat for 1 minute on each side, until cooked. Add a good scrunch of pepper, then add the chorizo cubes and fry for a further 2–3 minutes, turning and stirring everything often.

Remove the chorizo and scallops from the pan, and leave until cool enough to handle, then thread one scallop and chorizo cube onto a cocktail stick/toothpick. I recommend putting the scallop on first as the chorizo does a better job of gripping the stick.

Repeat to make 12 canapés in total. Serve immediately, while still warm, sprinkled with a little paprika, if you like.

Variation
You can always add a little chilli/chili powder or paprika to coat the scallops before cooking, but I find that enough flavourful oil comes out of good-quality chorizo as you fry it.

CORNICHONS WRAPPED IN SALAMI

As simple as the name suggests. These mini gherkins are often served with salami because the flavours complement each other perfectly. This combination really is a delight for the tastebuds – saltiness from the meat and acidity of the pickled cornichons (see page 135 for instructions on home pickling). If you put them side by side on the plate, nobody can resist rolling them up, so you might as well do the work for them!

12 slices salami

12 cornichons (or 12 small slices of pickled gherkin)

freshly ground black pepper

MAKES 12

For each bite, just wrap a slice of salami around a cornichon and pop a cocktail stick/toothpick through the middle to hold them together. Easy, right? I assure you, I spent only a proportionate amount of time on this recipe...

Repeat to make 12 bites in total. Crack a little pepper over the plate and serve.

MOZZARELLA PEARLS WRAPPED IN PROSCIUTTO

So simple, just like the recipe above. Don't use a whole slice of prosciutto per mini mozzarella pearl/ball, as that's a heavy mouthful, as well as being expensive for entertaining. I use kitchen scissors to cut each slice of prosciutto into quarters.

3 slices prosciutto

12 mini mozzarella pearls/balls

freshly ground black pepper

MAKES 12

Cut each slice of prosciutto lengthways in quarters (kitchen scissors are best for doing this) to make 12 strips in total. Wrap each strip around a mini mozzarella pearl/ball.

Pop a cocktail stick/toothpick through the middle of each assembled bite to hold it together, crack a little black pepper over the plate and serve.

CHORIZO AND CALAMARI 'PLANETS'

This is another recipe for a cocktail stick/toothpick canapé, but you lay them flat, like a chicken satay, for example. These are really simple and quick to do, especially if you use pre-cooked calamari. I think they look like planets, hence the name!

12 rings calamari/raw squid (or use cooked calamari)

12 x 1-cm/½-inch cubes chorizo

olive oil, for frying

MAKES 12

Heat a non-stick frying pan/skillet over medium heat. If you're using raw squid, place it in the hot pan with a little olive oil, and cook for about 8 minutes, until the rings have firmed up. Remove from the pan and allow to cool slightly.

Push a cube of chorizo into the middle of a calamari ring, then secure it in place with a cocktail stick/toothpick, pushing the cocktail stick/toothpick through the side of the calamari ring, through the chorizo in the middle and out the other side of the calamari ring. Repeat to make 12 canapés in total.

Lay the prepared canapés back in the hot frying pan/skillet and cook over medium heat for 2–3 minutes, until the chorizo starts to warm and soften and the oil produced from the chorizo coats the calamari. Serve immediately.

DEVILS ON HORSEBACK

There's a debate about when these bites had their 'heyday', which only means they've never gone away. So, let's keep the Devils on Horseback alive and cantering, and put a charcuterie spin on it!

6 slices prosciutto

12 whole blanched almonds

12 pitted dried dates or prunes

MAKES 12

Cut each slice of prosciutto lengthways down the middle (kitchen scissors work best for doing this) to make 12 half-slices.

For each 'devil', put an almond in the middle of a pitted date, wrap a half slice of prosciutto tightly around the fruit and then lay it on a baking sheet. Repeat to make 12 'devils' in total.

Preheat the grill/broiler to high.

Grill/broil the 'devils' for about 5 minutes, until the prosciutto starts to brown and crisp. Turn the 'devils' over and grill/broil for a further 2–3 minutes. Push a cocktail stick/toothpick through the middle of each one and serve immediately.

HORSES ON DEVILBACK

Huh? Horses on Devilback? Yes, fair's fair. It's the horse's turn now. I've recommended using saucisson sec or Serrano ham here because of their dark, rich flavour.

12 pitted prunes

12 slices saucisson sec or 6 slices Serrano ham

6 teaspoons mango chutney

MAKES 12

Make sure that the pitted prunes each have a hole that goes all the way through the middle. If you are using Serrano ham, cut each slice lengthways down the middle using scissors to make 12 half-slices.

For each 'horse', take a slice of saucisson sec or a half-slice of Serrano ham. Spread ½ teaspoon mango chutney over each slice of meat, then roll the meat into a tight tube, and thread it through the middle of a prune. Lay it on a baking sheet. Repeat to make 12 'horses' in total.

Preheat the grill/broiler to high.

Grill/broil the 'horses' for about 2 minutes to warm them through, turning once. Push a cocktail stick/toothpick through the middle of each one and serve immediately.

ANGELS ON HORSEBACK

The mango chutney is optional here, but I like it because it adds sweetness to the salty first taste and softens the smokiness of the oysters. These are always a party favourite!

6 slices prosciutto

6 teaspoons mango chutney (optional)

12 smoked oysters

MAKES 12

Cut each slice of prosciutto lengthways down the middle to make 12 half-slices in total.

Spread ½ teaspoon mango chutney at one end of a half-slice of prosciutto. Place a smoked oyster on top and roll up the prosciutto around the oyster. Repeat to make 12 'angels' in total.

Heat a non-stick frying pan/skillet over medium heat until hot. Add the 'angels' to the pan. Cook them over medium heat for 1 minute, then turn over and cook for 1 minute more. This is merely to warm them through and release the flavour of the prosciutto.

Push a cocktail stick/toothpick through the middle of each one and serve immediately.

CHICKEN LIVER PÂTÉ

I have no idea why I grew up thinking that pâté was hard to make. It isn't. Even the hardened butter on the top used to look like a secret trick to perfect. It's not. The foundation of a simple chicken liver pâté can also be a great basis for some fun with additional flavours and ingredients. Here's a classic combination to get you started.

45 g/3½ tablespoons butter

2 shallots, chopped

1 garlic clove, chopped

75 g/3 oz. pork belly (rind removed), diced

200 g/7 oz. chicken livers, chopped

a pinch of freshly chopped thyme, plus extra to decorate

1 tablespoon brandy

2 bay leaves

a squeeze of fresh lemon juice (about 1 teaspoon)

sea salt and freshly ground black pepper

black and pink peppercorns, to decorate

Wholemeal Crispbread (see page 155) or Home-baked Oatcakes (see page 155), to serve

SERVES 4

Heat 20 g/generous 1 tablespoon of the butter in a frying pan/skillet over medium heat, until melted. Add the shallots and garlic and fry on their own for 1 minute. Add the pork belly, chicken livers, thyme and brandy, season with salt and pepper, and stir. Put the bay leaves on top and let them soften, if you are using dried ones. Cook, stirring regularly for 10 minutes, until everything is browned and the chicken livers are cooked through.

Remove from the heat and let cool until the mixture is warm, not hot – don't let it cool completely, otherwise the ingredients will dry out. Remove and discard the bay leaves.

Put the mixture into a food processor (don't wash the pan yet), add a squeeze of lemon juice and whizz. It's up to you how coarse you like it. I like a quite smooth pâté, so I process until the mixture sticks to the sides. You can also pulse for a short time and keep some chunks, if you prefer. Spoon the mixture into a dish (or into separate ramekins) and level the surface so that the melted butter can go on top.

In the same frying pan/skillet you were using before, melt the remaining butter over medium heat, until it starts to bubble, and then remove from the heat and pour over the top of the pâté. Decorate with a little extra thyme and some black and pink peppercorns. Move the pâté to the refrigerator and the butter will set in about 1 hour.

Serve with Wholemeal Crispbread or Home-baked Oatcakes, plus a little Fig Chutney (see page 146) to sweeten, if you like.

The pâté will keep in the refrigerator for 1 week, if the butter is unbroken on the top. Eat within 3 days once you have dipped through the surface. You can freeze the pâté in balls wrapped in clingfilm/plastic wrap (without the melted butter topping) and slowly defrost (do not reheat nor microwave). Once defrosted, you can transfer to ramekins and add the melted butter to the top.

PÂTÉ WITH DRIED APRICOTS AND PISTACHIOS

In this recipe, I have had a bit of fun with a classic pâté, and the results are delicious. The sweetness from the apricots is lovely alongside the richness of the chicken livers, and the texture, with the pistachio nuts, is really pleasing if you keep it chunky.

45 g/3½ tablespoons butter

½ red onion, chopped

½ garlic clove, chopped

75 g/3 oz. pork belly (rind removed), diced

200 g/7 oz. chicken livers, chopped

1 tablespoon brandy or Cointreau

60 g/2½ oz. ready-to-eat dried apricots, chopped

15 g/½ oz. shelled pistachio nuts

a squeeze of fresh lemon juice (about 1 teaspoon)

sea salt and freshly ground black pepper

finely sliced dready-to-eat dried apricots and pistachios, to decorate

Home-baked Oatcakes (see page 155) or Wholemeal Crispbread (see page 155), to serve

SERVES 4

Heat 20 g/generous 1 tablespoon of the butter in a frying pan/skillet over medium heat, until melted. Add the red onion and garlic, and fry on their own for 1 minute. Add the pork belly, chicken livers and brandy, season with salt and pepper, and stir. Cook, stirring regularly for 10 minutes, until everything is browned and the pork belly and chicken livers are cooked through.

Remove from the heat and let cool until the mixture is warm, not hot – don't let it cool completely, otherwise the ingredients will dry out.

Put the mixture into a food processor (don't wash the pan yet), add the apricots, pistachio nuts and the squeeze of lemon juice, and whizz. I like to keep this mixture chunky so that you still get a bite of apricot and the soft crunch of pistachio in the pâté. However, you can blitz until smooth, if you prefer. Spoon the mixture into a dish (or into separate ramekins) and level the surface so that the melted butter can go on top.

In the same frying pan/skillet you were using before, melt the remaining butter over medium heat, until it starts to bubble, and then remove from the heat and pour over the top of the pâté. Decorate with slices of dried apricot and and piastachios. Move the pâté to the refrigerator and the butter will set in about 1 hour.

Serve with Home-baked Oatcakes or Wholemeal Crispbread.

The pâté will keep in the refrigerator for 1 week, if the butter is unbroken on the top. Eat within 3 days once you have dipped through the surface. You can freeze the pâté in balls wrapped in clingfilm/plastic wrap (without the melted butter topping) and slowly defrost (do not reheat nor microwave). Once defrosted, you can transfer to ramekins and add the melted butter to the top.

DRIED CRANBERRY AND BRANDY CHRISTMAS PÂTÉ

A Christmas-themed pâté to serve at a seasonal gathering – or to keep in the refrigerator and nibble on at intervals, which is allowed at Christmastime, of course.

45 g/3½ tablespoons butter

2 shallots, chopped

1 garlic clove, chopped

2 tablespoons brandy

75 g/3 oz. pork belly (rind removed), diced

150 g/5 oz. chicken livers, chopped

a pinch of ground cloves

50 g/2 oz. dried cranberries, chopped, plus extra to decorate

a squeeze of fresh lemon juice (about 1 teaspoon)

sea salt and freshly ground black pepper

Melba Toast, to serve (see page 157)

SERVES 4

Heat 20 g/generous 1 tablespoon of the butter in a frying pan/skillet over medium heat, until melted. Add the shallots and garlic, and fry on their own for 1 minute. Add the brandy and cook for 1 minute, then add the pork belly, chicken livers and cloves, season with salt and pepper, and stir. Cook, stirring regularly for 10 minutes, until everything is browned and the pork belly and chicken livers are cooked through.

Remove from the heat and let cool until the mixture is warm, not hot – don't let it cool completely, otherwise the ingredients will dry out.

Put the mixture into a food processor (don't wash the pan yet), add the cranberries and the squeeze of lemon juice, and whizz. It's up to you how coarse you like it. I like quite a smooth pâté so I process until the mixture sticks to the sides. You can also pulse for a short time and keep some chunks, if you prefer. Spoon the mixture into a dish (or into separate ramekins) and level the surface so that the melted butter can go on top.

In the same frying pan/skillet you were using before, melt the remaining butter over medium heat, until it starts to bubble, and then remove from the heat and pour over the top of the pâté. Decorate with dried cranberries. Move the pâté to the refrigerator and the butter will set in about 1 hour.

Serve with Melba Toast.

The pâté will keep in the refrigerator for 1 week, if the butter is unbroken on the top. Eat within 3 days once you have dipped through the surface. You can freeze the pâté in balls wrapped in clingfilm/plastic wrap (without the melted butter topping) and slowly defrost (do not reheat nor microwave). Once defrosted, you can transfer to ramekins and add the melted butter to the top.

PÂTÉ DE CAMPAGNE

This is not technically a pâté, but is similar to the Pork Rillettes on page 42, in that it is served like one. This recipe needs to be made the day before serving.

30 g/2 tablespoons butter

2 tablespoons brandy

4 shallots, finely chopped

1 garlic clove, finely chopped

1 egg

4 tablespoons double/heavy cream

½ teaspoon Dijon mustard

a pinch of fresh thyme leaves

400 g/14 oz. pork loin or shoulder (as much fat removed as possible), trimmed and cut into 1-cm/½-inch dice

6 slices prosciutto

100 g/3½ oz. ham hock, chopped (optional)

hard-boiled egg, peeled (optional)

sea salt and freshly ground black pepper

20 x 10-cm/8 x 4-inch loaf pan, greased

SERVES 4/MAKES 1 LOAF

Preheat the oven to 180°C (350°F) Gas 4.

Melt the butter in a frying pan/skillet over medium heat, then add the brandy. Let it boil and reduce for a minute, then add the shallots and garlic. Once those have softened, remove the frying pan/skillet from the heat and let cool.

In a bowl, beat the egg and then stir in the cream, mustard and thyme, and season with salt and pepper. Add the diced pork, then stir in the cooled shallot mixture and any juices from the pan.

Lay the slices of prosciutto across the bottom and up the sides of the prepared loaf pan so that they line the pan. I recommend leaving just a small gap between the slices so that the loaf is easier to slice once it's cooked and then chilled. Spoon half of the pork mixture into the pan and then sprinkle the ham hock pieces across the middle, if using. You can have a bit of fun here by placing a peeled hard-boiled egg in the middle. It looks attractive when sliced.

Spoon the remaining pork mixture on top and then fold in the ends of the prosciutto, if the slices are longer than the inside surface of the loaf pan. Cover the pan tightly with foil. Take a larger roasting dish and put 2.5 cm/1 inch of water in the bottom. Lower the loaf pan into the water and cook in the preheated oven for 1 hour, until the mixture around the meat has thickened and the meat is firm to the touch. Remove the loaf pan from the water bath and let cool for 30 minutes.

The loaf pan should now be cool enough to move to the refrigerator to finish setting. The pâté will take a good few hours to set properly, which is why I recommend making it the day before.

Like with the Pork Rillettes recipe, I wouldn't serve this straight from the refrigerator. I let it come to room temperature for about 20–30 minutes before serving. Serve it with the Home-baked Oatcakes (see page 155) or Garlic-y Bruschetta (see page 156).

When it comes to serving, just run a knife around the edge of the loaf to release it from the sides of the pan and then turn it out onto a board. You'll now see what I mean about leaving the small gap between the prosciutto so that you can slice the softer mixture below it without dragging the prosciutto with your knife.

This pâté is heavenly served with an ice-cold glass of dry white wine like Sancerre and maybe a game of pétanque in a French courtyard!

PORK RILLETTES

Rillettes are like a pâté with a bit more texture, because the meat is shredded, rather than puréed. Best served at room temperature, with some Melba toast or crispbread, this is a special and flavourful appetizer or canapé, and very easy to make.

200 g/7 oz. pork belly (rindless), trimmed and diced

1 tablespoon sea salt

30 g/2 tablespoons butter

1 garlic clove, finely chopped

a small pinch of ground mace

1 bay leaf

a pinch of freshly chopped or dried parsley

50 ml/scant ¼ cup dry white wine

150 ml/⅔ cup chicken stock

sea salt and freshly ground black pepper

freshly squeezed lemon juice and freshly chopped parsley, to serve (optional)

Melba Toast, to serve (see page 157)

SERVES 2

Put the pork belly in a non-metallic container and sprinkle the salt over the top. Massage the salt into the meat, then cover tightly and refrigerate for 1–2 hours. Rinse and dry the pork cubes – the salt should have already drawn some of the moisture out of the pork belly, but you don't want to draw out too much because you're going to slow-cook it, which will benefit from keeping the fat.

Melt the butter in a saucepan over medium heat (you're going to need a saucepan with a lid), then add the pork belly, garlic, mace, bay leaf and parsley, and season with salt and pepper. Cook, stirring often, to slightly brown the pork and coat it in the seasoning, then add the white wine and keep increase the heat to high for 1–2 minutes to reduce the wine. Pour in the chicken stock.

Turn the heat down to very low and put the lid on the pan. Leave it cooking gently for 1¼ hours. At this stage, press one of the cubes of pork with a fork and if it starts to fall apart, it's had long enough. However, it's likely that it'll need a little longer. If the mixture is starting to dry out and stick to the bottom of the pan, just add another splash of chicken stock – about 50 ml/scant ¼ cup. Replace the lid and leave to cook gently for another 20–30 minutes, until the meat is falling apart.

Remove from the heat and leave to cool. Discard the bay leaf.

The best way to shred the pork is with your fingers, so let it cool enough to touch, then pull it apart with your fingers and mix it really well. If you have a large piece of fat on its own, you can remove it, but the fat should have mostly melted.

Transfer the pork to a container or 2 ramekins and chill in the refrigerator for at least 1 hour so that the mixture can set.

I recommend bringing it out of the refrigerator about 30 minutes before serving – the texture of shredded meat is best at room temperature and it allows the flavour to come through really well. Feel free to add a squeeze of lemon juice before serving, an extra crack of black pepper and a sprinkling of freshly chopped parsley, if you like.

Cook's Note
This recipe uses pork belly but the same process works well with duck, pheasant and venison. If you're using venison, which is very lean, I recommend adding 100 g/3¼ oz. pork belly (rindless) to it for extra flavour. You can use beef too; diced sirloin or rib-eye steak works well.

'SUSHI STYLE' PROSCIUTTO-WRAPPED GOATS' CHEESE AND ROCKET

Sushi was another triumph in man's battle against shelf-life. Like salumi, the method of fermenting fish with rice and vinegars was designed to extend the life of the fish. Before methods were developed to make the rice and wrapping just as delicious as the fish in the middle, the rice was discarded before the fish was eaten. So, as a tribute to our ancestors' peers in the Far East, here's a sushi-inspired recipe using charcuterie.

12 slices prosciutto

3 tablespoons Puttanesca Relish
(see page 148)

a handful of rocket/arugula
(about 4–5 leaves per roll)

200 g/7 oz. goats' cheese, sliced
into 12 strips (or cheese of your
choice; Gorgonzola is good too)

MAKES 24

Lay a slice of prosciutto flat on a board or plate. Spread 1 teaspoon of the relish over the surface. Sprinkle 4–5 rocket/arugula leaves on the top, then put a strip of cheese on top in the middle.

Roll the prosciutto over on itself to enclose the filling, like a 'nori roll', and then slice (it is easiest to snip with kitchen scissors) in half to create two circles. Push a cocktail stick/toothpick through each assembled bite to hold it together.

Repeat to make 24 bites in total. Serve immediately.

Alternatively, roll each slice of prosciutto with its filling into a cone so it's wider at the top, like 'temaki'. You will make 12 larger bites using this method.

PARMA HAM AND MELON

This is such a classic appetizer and what it lacks in imagination and flair, it gains in everyone still having plenty of room for a lovely big main course/entrée. So don't knock it until you've had seconds of pudding, when you'll thank it. I've a take on it though, which I prefer to melon. Traditional recipe first:

8 slices Parma ham

½ melon, peeled, deseeded and sliced into thin slices

4 squeezes of fresh lime juice

4 pinches of freshly ground black pepper

SERVES 4

Divide the ham and melon evenly between the serving plates. Either place the Parma ham and melon neatly on the plate next to each other or wrap the Parma ham around the slices of melon. Squeeze lime juice over the top of each serving and sprinkle with pepper.

PARMA HAM AND GRAPEFRUIT

8 white
grapefruit
segments

8 pink
grapefruit
segments

8 tablespoons
sloe gin (or
other fruit
liqueur)

8 slices
Parma ham

SERVES 4

With this alternative recipe, I recommend serving the grapefruit segments and Parma ham next to each other, rather than wrapping the Parma ham around the grapefruit. I only say this because I find tastebuds need to prepare themselves for grapefruit, even sweetened grapefruit like this. Your companions will instinctively put the right balance of the sour and salty on their fork to suit their own taste buds. We do this the whole time, we don't even realise it.

Put the grapefruit segments into a bowl, pour over the sloe gin and leave to soak for at least 1 hour, but ideally for 3–4 hours. Serve with the Parma ham, allowing 4 grapefruit segments (plus some sloe gin) and 2 slices of Parma ham per serving.

PIZZETTES

These are mini pizzas. They're quite filling, so they're ideal for a drinks party when you have no intention of keeping your guests for dinner. Or they can be an appetizer if your main course/entrée isn't too heavy. They are also useful for lunch menus if you serve two together or make slightly larger ones, and make great children's party food.

FOR THE BASE/CRUST

170 g/1½ cups plain/all-purpose or wholemeal/whole-wheat flour

a small pinch of fast-action/rapid-rise yeast

1 tablespoon olive oil

a pinch of sea salt

1 teaspoon caster/granulated sugar

FOR THE TOPPING

1 tablespoon olive oil

300 g/11 oz. pancetta, thinly sliced or diced

400-g/14-oz. can of tomatoes, drained and chopped

a big pinch of freshly chopped parsley

a big pinch of freshly chopped or dried oregano

1 tablespoon tomato purée/paste

about 40 g/1½ oz. Caramelized Red Onions (see page 147) (optional)

200 g/7 oz. pecorino or Parmesan cheese, grated or shaved

sea salt and freshly ground black pepper

a large baking sheet, greased or lined with parchment paper

MAKES 6 PIZZETTES

Preheat the oven to 180°C (350°F) Gas 4.

For the base/crust, put all the ingredients in a bowl, add 125 ml/½ cup water and mix together with your hands to make a dough. If the mixture feels sloppy, just add a little more flour, or add a little more water for the opposite (it shouldn't be so dry that it crumbles when you roll it). Turn the dough out onto a flour-dusted surface and knead for 5–10 minutes, until smooth and elastic. The kneading is always a bit boring but just remember that you need (groan!) to do it or your base will be chewy and tough. If you have a bread maker, it will do the work for you – just follow the timing instructions for your machine.

Divide the dough into six even pieces. On a flour-dusted surface, roll out each portion of dough into an oval. Place the pizza bases/crusts on the prepared baking sheet and bake in the preheated oven for 10 minutes, turning over halfway through.

Meanwhile, prepare the topping. Heat the olive oil in a frying pan/skillet. Add the pancetta and fry over medium heat, until fully cooked – let it brown but don't reduce it right down at this stage because it will continue to bake on top of the pizzettes. Put the canned tomatoes, parsley, oregano and tomato purée/paste into a bowl, season with salt and pepper, and mix well.

Once the pizza bases/crusts are initially baked, remove from the oven. Spread the tomato mixture over the top of the bases/crusts and then spoon over the caramelized onions, if using. Put the pancetta pieces on top, then sprinkle over the cheese.

Return the pizzettes to the preheated oven on the middle shelf (ideally, put the pizzettes directly onto the oven shelf, rather than using the baking sheet, so the bases can continue to crisp) and bake for a further 15 minutes, until the cheese has melted. Serve hot.

CURED DUCK AND MUSTARD BRUSCHETTA

For home-curing your own duck breast, see page 129. Otherwise, you could use slices of any cured meats. I'd recommend a good, rich cured meat – cured mutton is ideal if you can buy it, or cured venison is delicious and very lean.

4 slices Garlic-y Bruschetta (see page 156)

about 2 teaspoons wholegrain mustard (Dijon/French or English/hot mustard also work well)

a handful of rocket/arugula leaves

12 slices cured duck breast (see page 129)

MAKES 4

For the bruschetta, see the Garlic-y Bruschetta recipe on page 156.

Spread some mustard on each slice of bruschetta. Arrange a few leaves of rocket/arugula on the top and layer the slices of cured meat over the top. Serve immediately.

If your bruschetta slice is larger than bite-size, or if you're not eating it with a knife and fork, I recommend cutting each slice of cured meat into 2 or 3 smaller pieces. This is just because if you pick it up and bite it, you'll probably pull the whole slice of meat off with the first mouthful and the rest of your bruschetta will never be the same!

'SCOTCH EGGS'

This is a take on traditional Scotch eggs for a little canapé. It's a very easy version to prepare too.

12 quail's eggs

6 slices prosciutto, coppa or Serrano ham

sea salt and freshly ground black pepper

MAKES 12

Hard-boil/hard-cook the quail's eggs in a pan of boiling water for 5 minutes. Drain and plunge the eggs into cold water, then drain again and let cool. Remove the shells, dry the eggs with paper towels and then roll them in salt and freshly ground black pepper.

Cut each slice of cured ham lengthways down the middle (kitchen scissors are easiest for doing this) to make 12 half-slices in total.

Roll each quail's egg up inside a half-slice of ham. You might need to insert a cocktail stick/toothpick through each canapé if the quail's eggs are bigger, but they'll hold together by themselves if they're small. Serve immediately.

MILLIONAIRE'S FINGER FOOD

This is one of the more unusual conversation-starters at a drinks party: "Do you know, that mouthful costs more per kg/lb than 9-carat gold...!"

The process of making charcuterie is long and very expensive. Jamón Ibérico de Bellota, which I briefly cover in the introduction section for the Spanish section of the Charcuterie Board chapter, takes more than four years to produce and has pigs roaming around forests getting fat on acorns. This particular example is one of the most expensive foods (let alone meats) that one can buy.

So, if you fold some of that on a cocktail stick/toothpick with a small spoonful of black truffle pâté (foie gras is even slightly more expensive, but I confidently denounce the process), and serve with a little pot of mayonnaise seasoned with saffron and lime, you have a very valuable mouthful indeed. You would need only a tiny amount of saffron and a small piece of the ham and the truffle pâté but still, it's a pretty swanky way to start a drinks party, isn't it?

12 small strips jamón Ibérico

3 teaspoons black truffle pâté

FOR THE SAFFRON MAYONNAISE

4 tablespoons good-quality mayonnaise

a pinch of saffron (about 8 strands)

a squeeze of fresh lime juice

sea salt and freshly ground black pepper

MAKES 12

To make each one of these tasty morsels, wrap a small strip of jamón Ibérico around ¼ teaspoon black truffle pâté. Repeat to make 12 tasty morsels in total.

Put a cocktail stick/toothpick through the middle of each one to hold the ham in place. Alternatively, for elegant presentation, use dainty little forks instead.

These are delicious dipped into saffron mayonnaise. It is quick and easy to make – mix the mayonnaise with the saffron and a squeeze of lime juice, then season to taste with salt and pepper.

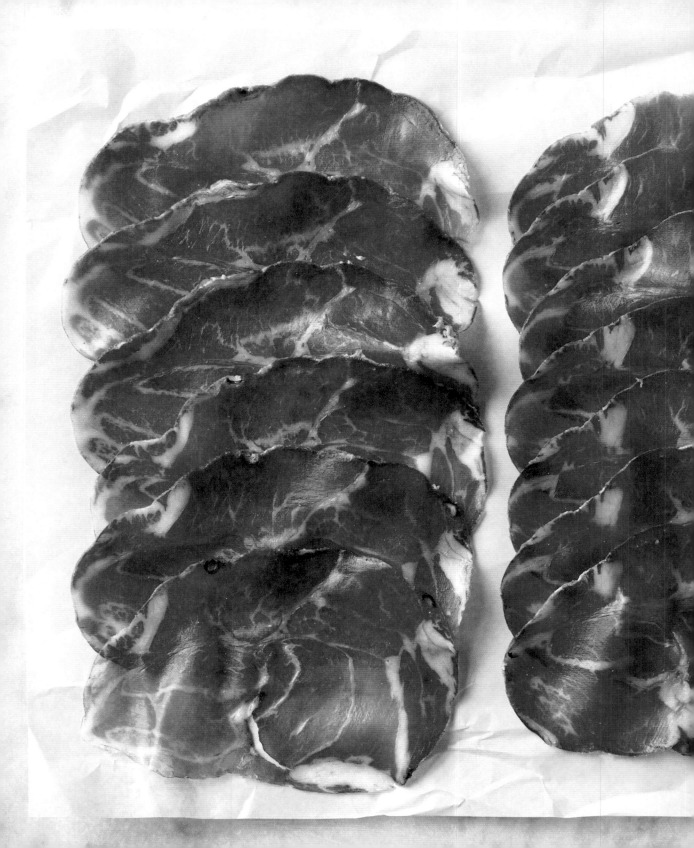

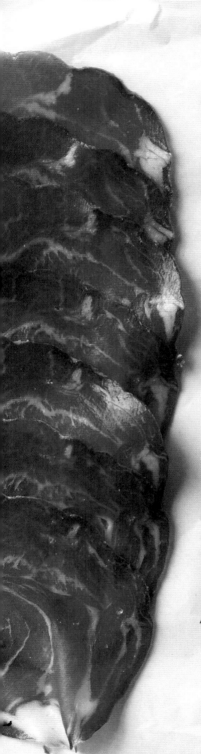

APPETIZERS, SALADS AND LIGHT LUNCHES

BRESAOLA, OVEN TOMATOES AND BUFFALO MOZZARELLA SALAD, WITH MUSTARD DRESSING

Bresaola is probably the best-known cured beef and I think it's a lovely way to enjoy beef. For many recipes, it combines even better with other flavours and ingredients than does cured pork, particularly in salads; it's generally a bit lighter in flavour and texture, so it works with the other ingredients rather than dominates them.

FOR THE SALAD

16–20 baby plum tomatoes, halved

1 tablespoon olive oil

a small bunch of fresh basil leaves (you want about 5–6 leaves per serving)

4 large handfuls of salad leaves/greens of your choice – I recommend a mixture of baby leaf spinach and rocket/arugula

165 g/5½ oz. buffalo mozzarella, drained and torn into pieces (or use 32–36 mini mozzarella pearls/balls)

165 g/5½ oz. bresaola slices (about 20 average slices)

sea salt and freshly ground black pepper

FOR THE MUSTARD DRESSING

2 tablespoons olive oil

2 tablespoons balsamic vinegar

1 tablespoon runny honey

1 teaspoon wholegrain mustard

SERVES 4

For the salad, first make the oven tomatoes. These tomatoes are best if made a day before, or at least given time to chill down in the refrigerator, so they become chewier and absorb the oil.

Preheat the oven to 180°C (350°F) Gas 4.

Put the halved tomatoes in a shallow ovenproof dish and drizzle the olive oil over the top. Tear the basil leaves over the tomatoes, then season with salt and pepper. Roast in the preheated oven for about 15–20 minutes, giving them a shimmy halfway through. Remove from the oven and let cool, then refrigerate.

When you are ready to serve, make the mustard dressing by simply combining the olive oil, vinegar, honey and mustard in a bowl, seasoning with salt and pepper, and mixing well.

Dress the salad leaves/greens with most of the dressing (reserving a little dressing for drizzling on top) and divide between 4 serving plates, then pop the torn mozzarella (or 8–9 mini mozzarella pearls/balls per serving), chilled oven tomatoes and bresaola slices (see Cook's Note) on top, dividing them evenly between each plate. Drizzle the salads with the remaining dressing so that you get a taste of it even with the first mouthful, and serve immediately.

Cook's Note

It's always a shame to tear cured meat on top of salads, because it doesn't look as pretty. However, remember that cured meat like bresaola doesn't cut very easily, so if someone is just using a fork to eat the salad, they're only going to get 5 big mouthfuls of bresaola and then no more. Therefore, for the price of a little presentation, I would tear the bresaola into smaller pieces so it's distributed evenly for every mouthful.

PROSCIUTTO, ARTICHOKE, FIG AND ROQUEFORT SALAD WITH BALSAMIC DRESSING

A lovely, light summer salad – sweetness in the fig, saltiness in the prosciutto, and creamy Roquefort. A really simple balsamic dressing is fine for this one too, as there are already plenty of flavours in the salad.

FOR THE SALAD

60 g/4 tablespoons butter

4 fresh figs (skin on), quartered

4 large handfuls of salad leaves/greens of your choice (Little Gem/Bibb lettuce is very good for this salad)

125 g/4¼ oz. Roquefort cheese, crumbled

16–20 cooked artichoke hearts, chopped (I use the marinated artichoke hearts sold in jars)

165 g/5½ oz. prosciutto slices (about 20 average slices)

a small bunch of fresh basil leaves (about 5–6 leaves per serving)

sea salt and freshly ground black pepper

FOR THE DRESSING

2 tablespoons olive oil

1 tablespoon balsamic vinegar

SERVES 4

Preheat the grill/broiler to high.

For the salad, rub a little butter on all the cut surfaces of the figs, put them on a baking sheet, cut-sides up, and then pop them under the preheated grill/broiler for 6–8 minutes, turning once. Let them soften and start to brown, but don't let them shrivel up too much. Remove from the heat.

Meanwhile, make the dressing by combining the olive oil and vinegar in a bowl, seasoning with salt and pepper, and mixing well.

Dress the salad leaves/greens with most of the dressing (reserving a little dressing for drizzling on top) and divide between 4 serving plates, then pop the Roquefort, grilled figs, artichokes, prosciutto slices (see Cook's Note) and basil leaves on top, dividing them evenly between each plate. Drizzle the salads with the remaining dressing and serve immediately.

Cook's Note

Like with the Bresaola, Oven Tomatoes and Buffalo Mozzarella Salad with Mustard Dressing on page 59, it's always a shame to tear cured meat on top of salads because it doesn't look very pretty. However, remember that cured meat like prosciutto doesn't cut very easily, so if someone is just using a fork to eat the salad, they're only going to get 5 big mouthfuls of prosciutto and then no more. Therefore, for the price of a little presentation, I would tear the prosciutto into smaller pieces so it's distributed evenly for every mouthful.

PANCETTA, BRUSSELS SPROUT, CHESTNUT AND CAMEMBERT CHRISTMAS SALAD WITH CRANBERRY SAUCE

It's a good idea to schedule at least one salad into the Christmas season menu... but that doesn't mean it has to be a flimsy salad. Why not combine lots of the classic Christmas flavours or leftovers in a delicious salad?

125 g/4¼ oz. pancetta, finely diced (use Home-cured Pancetta on page 126, if you like)

4 handfuls of Brussels sprouts (about 165 g/5½ oz. in total), trimmed and halved

60 g/4 tablespoons butter

12–16 roasted chestnuts, peeled (see Cook's Note)

125 g/4¼ oz. Camembert, torn into pieces

sea salt and freshly ground black pepper

Romano lettuce leaves (or another soft leaf, like Lollo rosso) and cranberry sauce, to serve

olive oil, to drizzle

SERVES 4

Start by frying the pancetta in a hot frying pan/skillet until it's crisp and browned. Remove from the pan to a plate, but don't worry about washing up the frying pan/skillet just yet.

At the same time, steam (or boil) the Brussels sprouts over (or in) a separate pan of boiling water for 5 minutes, until they soften. Drain and set aside.

Once you've removed the pancetta from the frying pan/skillet, add the butter to melt (and mix with the oils from the pancetta), then add the Brussels sprouts and chestnuts and mix well to coat in the buttery juices. Remove from the heat and season with salt and pepper.

For each serving, lay some lettuce leaves in each serving bowl, then put everything on top (pancetta, Brussels sprouts and chestnuts, and finally the Camembert), dividing the ingredients evenly between the bowls. Add a dollop of cranberry sauce on top of each portion and a drizzle of olive oil to dress. Crunch plenty of black pepper over the top and serve immediately.

Cook's Note
You can roast your own chestnuts for this recipe, or use ready-roasted.

BROAD BEAN, PEA, MINT, GOATS' CHEESE AND FRIED PANCETTA SALAD

There is only one taste experience that can equal squeezing broad/fava beans fresh from the pod straight into your mouth... and that's making them all warm and buttery and mixing them with pancetta. This recipe is all about the freshness of flavour in broad/fava beans, peas and mint, and mixing them with the richness of goats' cheese and pancetta to turn this from a side salad into a light meal.

125 g/4¼ oz. pancetta, finely diced

400 g/14 oz. broad/fava beans, shelled

200 g/scant 2 cups fresh or frozen peas

60 g/4 tablespoons butter

2 garlic cloves, finely chopped

a small handful of fresh mint leaves (about 12–16 leaves), chopped

1 tablespoon freshly chopped parsley

freshly squeezed juice of ½ lemon

125 g/4¼ oz. soft goats' cheese, torn into chunks

sea salt and freshly ground black pepper

SERVES 4

Start by frying the pancetta in a hot frying pan/skillet until it's crisp and browned. Remove from the pan to a plate, but don't worry about washing up the frying pan/skillet just yet.

At the same time, steam (or boil) the broad/fava beans and peas over (or in) a separate pan of boiling water for 4 minutes, until the broad/fava beans soften. Drain and set aside.

Once you've removed the pancetta from the pan, add the butter to melt (and mix with the oils from the pancetta), then add the garlic and allow that to brown, stirring often. Add the broad/fava beans, peas, mint, parsley, lemon juice and a pinch of salt, and mix well.

Remove from the heat and transfer to a salad bowl. Put the goats' cheese and pancetta on top. Crunch plenty of black pepper over and serve immediately.

SERRANO HAM, PINE NUT, LETTUCE AND PARMESAN WRAPS

These wraps make a great packed lunch; they are delicious served still warm at home too.

8 small handfuls of pine nuts

8 soft flour tortillas

8 slices Serrano ham (or use prosciutto, if you prefer)

1 Romano lettuce, shredded

125 g/4¼ oz. Parmesan cheese shavings

3–4 tablespoons garlic mayonnaise

sea salt and freshly ground black pepper

MAKES 8 WRAPS

Heat a dry frying pan/skillet over high heat, until hot, then add the pine nuts and cook for 3–4 minutes, until the pine nuts are lightly toasted. Remove the pine nuts from the pan and set aside.

Put the tortillas into the same pan, one at a time, for about 20 seconds each, until warm.

Lay the warm tortillas on a board or plate and put a slice of ham flat on top of each one. Put some shredded lettuce, Parmesan shavings and toasted pine nuts in the middle of each tortilla on top of the ham, dividing them evenly between each portion. Spoon a little garlic mayonnaise on the top of each and season with salt and pepper.

Fold each tortilla around the filling to make a wrap (fold up the bottom first so that the pine nuts don't drop out at the bottom). Serve immediately or let cool for a couple of minutes before wrapping in foil to take with you for a picnic or lunch.

Variation
You can use Caesar-style salad dressing or crème fraîche/sour cream instead of the mayonnaise, if you prefer.

TAPAS

Chorizo is, of course, one of the most popular cured meat products from Spain, and Spain's wonderful tradition of tapas celebrates chorizo in some delicious ways.

PROSCIUTTO AND CHORIZO CROQUETAS

50 g/3½ tablespoons butter

140 g/generous 1 cup plain/all-purpose flour, plus 50 g/scant ½ cup

300 ml/1¼ cups full-fat/whole milk

50 g/2 oz. chorizo, finely chopped

4 slices prosciutto, shredded

a big pinch of freshly chopped parsley

a pinch of dried chilli/hot pepper flakes (optional)

2 eggs, beaten

75 g/generous 1 cup fresh breadcrumbs

sea salt and freshly ground black pepper

olive oil, for frying

MAKES 10

To make the croquetas, melt the butter in a frying pan/skillet and then stir in the 140 g/generous 1 cup flour. Cook for 2 minutes, then slowly add the milk, a little at a time, stirring constantly. Cook for a couple of minutes, until thick, then mix in the chorizo, prosciutto, parsley, chilli/hot pepper flakes, if using, and some salt and pepper.

Remove from the heat and let cool slightly, then cover with clingfilm/plastic wrap and chill in the refrigerator for 2 hours.

Form the chilled croqueta mixture into 10 little balls or sausage shapes. Put the remaining 50 g/scant ½ cup flour in a bowl or shallow dish. Dip your hands in the flour, pick up a shaped croqueta, roll it in the flour to coat, then dip it in the beaten eggs. Finally, coat it well in breadcrumbs. Repeat with all the croquetas.

Meanwhile, heat a few centimetres/inches of olive oil in a heavy-based saucepan until hot (heat enough oil to come as high as at least half the height of the croquetas in your pan). Fry the coated croquetas in the hot oil, in batches, for about 10 minutes, until they are crisp and golden all over, turning occasionally. Remove from the oil using a slotted spoon and drain on paper towels. Serve hot.

RED WINE CHORIZO

165 g/5½ oz. chorizo, sliced

olive oil, for frying (optional)

160 ml/⅔ cup red wine

SERVES 4

Heat a frying pan/skillet until hot, then add the chorizo slices and fry for 2–3 minutes, turning regularly, until they have browned on both sides and have shrunk slightly. If you have a good non-stick frying pan/skillet, you won't need oil before you put the chorizo in. If you are worried about the chorizo sticking, just add a drop or two of olive oil to the pan. The chorizo will release a lot of oils when cooked and that's the flavour we want.

Carefully pour the red wine into the pan over the chorizo slices and keep stirring. Cook for 2–3 minutes over medium heat, until the red wine starts to reduce. Continue to cook until the wine has thickened and become sticky.

Remove from the heat and transfer the mixture to a dish. Serve.

COJUNUDO

I like this name for tapas because the word is used in Spanish for when we would say 'awesome' or, for food, 'delicious', and the origin of the word comes from complimenting a man on his sexual prowess. Seems a good enough reason to serve this dish to me!

125 g/4¼ oz. chorizo, sliced

olive oil, for frying (optional)

4 slices pan rustico (or bread of your choice)

4 quail's eggs

freshly ground black pepper

freshly chopped parsley, to garnish

SERVES 4

Heat a frying pan/skillet over medium heat, add the chorizo slices to the pan and fry for 2–3 minutes, turning regularly, until they're browned on both sides. If you have a good non-stick frying pan/skillet, you won't need oil before you put the chorizo in. If you are worried about the chorizo sticking, just add a drop or two of olive oil to the pan. The chorizo will release a lot of oils when cooked. Remove the chorizo slices from the pan to a plate and set aside.

Fry the slices of bread in the same pan, on both sides, to soak up the oils from the chorizo, then transfer to serving plates and set aside.

Crack the quail's eggs into the pan and fry until cooked to your liking. Serve the eggs and chorizo slices on top of the slices of fried bread. Scrunch a little pepper on top, garnish with parsley and serve.

BRUSCHETTA WITH CHORIZO STRIPS, GRILLED RED PEPPER AND WATERCRESS

This is one of those appetizers or light lunches that you start politely eating with a knife and fork and are relieved when someone (usually me) picks it up in one hand and eats it like a big biscuit. It's jolly easy to make too.

4 x 5-cm/2-inch lengths of chorizo

1 red/bell pepper, deseeded

1 teaspoon olive oil

4 small handfuls of watercress (or salad leaves/greens of your choice)

4 slices Garlic-y Bruschetta (see page 156)

freshly ground black pepper

SERVES 4

Preheat the grill/broiler to high.

First, slice the chorizo pieces in half lengthways to make a total of 8 halves. Set aside.

Cut the red/bell pepper into quarters and then cut each quarter into quarters again, making them as flat as you can. Rub the olive oil all over the red/bell pepper pieces, then put them in a single layer on a baking sheet along with the halved chorizo pieces.

Pop the red/bell pepper and chorizo pieces under the preheated grill/broiler for 5–6 minutes, until the red/bell pepper is starting to brown on the edges and become soft. Remove from the heat.

For each serving, put a small handful of watercress on top of a slice of bruschetta and then layer 2 pieces of chorizo and 4 pieces of grilled/broiled red/bell pepper on top. Add a good scrunch of pepper to each serving. You probably won't need salt with the chorizo, but add it if you like. Serve immediately.

SERRANO HAM AND AUBERGINE OPEN SANDWICH

I find that I'm having open sandwiches quite often these days. I think it's because I can get more on the plate, so it's just a gluttonous thing. They're also great if you're entertaining at lunchtime, if you want something a bit fancier than a plain sandwich.

8 thin (5-mm/¼-inch thick) slices
aubergine/eggplant

olive oil, for brushing

4 slices fresh soda bread or crusty
wholemeal/whole-wheat bread
(or a base of your choice – toasted
English muffins also work well)

Puttanesca Relish (see page 148),
for spreading, or use a condiment
of your choice

8 slices Serrano ham (or use coppa
or prosciutto, if you prefer)

fresh parsley, for snipping

sea salt and freshly ground black
pepper

MAKES 4

Preheat the grill/broiler to high.

Put the aubergine/eggplant slices in a single layer on a baking sheet. Brush olive oil on both sides of the slices so that they're well covered, then sprinkle with salt and pepper on both sides. Grill/broil under the preheated grill/broiler for 5 minutes on each side, turning once. Remove from the heat.

Meanwhile, lightly toast the bread base, or leave it untoasted, if you prefer.

For each open sandwich, put a good spread of the relish on a slice of bread or toast. Put 2 grilled/broiled aubergine/eggplant slices on top and then ruffle 2 slices of the Serrano ham along the top. (You can shred the ham first, if you prefer, or serve it with a knife and fork so that the ham doesn't tear off the top with the first bite.) Using kitchen scissors, snip some fresh parsley on top and add a little salt and pepper. Serve immediately.

Variation
You can add some grated Parmesan or pecorino cheese on top to make even more wonderfully rich and filling sandwiches, if you like.

MORTADELLA, OLIVE TAPENADE AND ROCKET SANDWICH

Mortadella has a tough time sometimes because it bears an unfortunate resemblance to pork luncheon meat. Please believe me when I say that's where the comparison ends; it tastes so much better and has a lovely, pure flavour and texture. This is another simple sandwich recipe combining some rich, dark flavours with the mortadella.

8 slices fresh bread of your choice

butter (at room temperature), for spreading

4 tablespoons Olive Tapenade (see page 148)

8 slices mortadella

a large handful of rocket/arugula

balsamic vinegar, to drizzle

MAKES 4 SANDWICHES

Lightly toast the slices of bread (or use them untoasted, if you prefer).

Spread butter over the toasted bread, then spread the olive tapenade over 4 of the slices. Add the slices of mortadella (2 slices per sandwich) – it's soft to bite so you won't need to shred it. Add some rocket/arugula to each and then a drizzle of balsamic vinegar.

Top each with a second piece of toasted, buttered bread to make 4 sandwiches. Serve immediately.

HOT PROSCIUTTO PARCELS STUFFED WITH GOATS' CHEESE AND FRESH BASIL

These can be served as a canapé, in groups of three for an appetizer, or on top of a salad.

12 slices prosciutto

125 g/generous ½ cup soft goats' cheese

24 fresh basil leaves

freshly ground black pepper

MAKES 12

For each prosciutto parcel, lay a slice of prosciutto flat and put a heaped teaspoonful of the goats' cheese at one end. Place 2 basil leaves on top and sprinkle with a pinch of pepper. Fold the prosciutto over so that the goats' cheese is wrapped tightly inside. Repeat to make 12 prosciutto parcels in total.

Heat a dry frying pan/skillet (there's no need for oil if it's non-stick) or griddle pan over medium heat, until hot. Put the prosciutto parcels in the hot pan and cook for about 2 minutes on each side.

Remove from the heat and let cool slightly to serve as finger food or put on top of a salad.

Variations

You can use coppa or Serrano ham instead of prosciutto, if you prefer.

Not a fan of goats' cheese? This recipe also works well with halloumi instead. Just slice the halloumi, pop it under a preheated hot grill/broiler for 4–5 minutes first until it's lightly tinged brown and then wrap the halloumi in the prosciutto slices with either the basil or fresh parsley, before cooking the parcels as above. The halloumi is a richer cheese, so you could add a squeeze of lemon juice or some balsamic vinegar on top, if you like.

CHORIZO AND RED CABBAGE SALAD

This salad is stunning due to its vibrant red colour. It's a lovely way to make cabbage exciting, as just a small amount of chorizo lends superb depth of flavour.

FOR THE SALAD

1 tablespoon olive oil

½ red cabbage, cored and sliced or shredded

150 g/5 oz. chorizo, peeled and diced

FOR THE DRESSING

3 tablespoons olive oil

1 tablespoon red wine vinegar

½ teaspoon garlic purée or crushed garlic

a big pinch of freshly chopped parsley

a pinch of freshly chopped or dried tarragon

1 teaspoon freshly squeezed lime juice

SERVES 2 FOR A LIGHT LUNCH

For the salad, heat the olive oil in a frying pan/skillet over medium heat, then add the red cabbage and fry until soft, stirring regularly. Add the chorizo and keep stirring for 2–3 minutes, so that the chorizo starts to cook and releases its oils.

Remove from the heat and let cool.

Meanwhile, put all the ingredients for the dressing into a bowl and mix together well.

Once the cabbage and chorizo mixture has cooled, pour over the dressing, toss to mix, and serve.

CHORIZO, AVOCADO AND POACHED EGG OPEN SANDWICH

This is another lovely, light lunch option and, as with the Parma Ham and Grapefruit recipe (see page 47), an open sandwich leaves a little wriggle room for individual tastebuds, so your companions can make up their own forkfuls.

4 eggs

4 x 5-cm/2-inch lengths of chorizo sticks, cut in half lengthways

olive oil, to drizzle (or butter, if preferred)

4 slices soda bread or crusty wholemeal/whole-wheat bread, lightly toasted (or a base of your choice – toasted English muffins also work well)

2 ripe avocado pears, halved, pitted and peeled

freshly ground black pepper

MAKES 4 OPEN
SANDWICHES

Poach the eggs to your liking in a pan of gently simmering water. Drain just before serving.

Meanwhile, put the chorizo slices into a dry frying pan/skillet and fry for a minute or so on either side to release the oils and to warm the chorizo through. Remove from the heat.

For each open sandwich, drizzle a little olive oil on the toasted bread (or spread with butter, if you prefer). Crush half an avocado onto it using a fork, then layer 2 chorizo slices on top of the avocado. Place a poached egg on top, scrunch some black pepper over and serve immediately.

Variation

Another option (omitting the eggs, olive oil and bread base) is to finely dice the chorizo, lightly fry it, mix it with the crushed avocados, and season with pepper. This can then be served with Wholemeal Crispbread (see page 155) or Home-baked Oatcakes (see page 155), like a meaty take on guacamole.

CHORIZO AND BEAN BURGER

I would find it impossible to compile any collection of recipes without including a beloved burger (and do a little new product development in the process!). Having always enjoyed the flavour combination of beef and pork, I love the mixture of fresh minced/ground beef with a cured pork, like chorizo.

FOR THE BURGERS

400 g/14 oz. lean minced/ground beef

125 g/4½ oz. chorizo, finely diced

80 g/3¼ oz. canned red kidney beans (drained weight), rinsed, drained and crushed

60 g/2¼ oz. breadcrumbs

4 teaspoons tomato purée/paste

1 teaspoon freshly chopped parsley

sea salt and freshly ground black pepper

TO SERVE

4 crusty bread rolls or toasted English muffins, halved

salad leaves/greens

Puttanesca Relish (see page 148), Sweet Chilli Sticky Sweetcorn (see page 142) or Caramelized Red Onions (see page 147)

SERVES 4 (MAKES 4 CHUNKY 175 G/6 OZ. BURGERS)

Put all the burger ingredients in a large bowl and mix together really well with your hands. Divide the mixture into 4 and then shape each portion into a burger.

To cook the burgers, fry them in a frying pan/skillet over medium heat for 12–15 minutes, turning a few times, until cooked through. Alternatovely, pop them on the rack in a grill/broiler pan and cook under a preheated hot grill/broiler for 6 minutes on each side, until cooked through.

Serve the hot burgers in the bread rolls with some salad leaves/greens and the condiment of your choice.

SLICED COPPA AND SPRING ONION FRITTATA

Frittata – the Italian omelette. This can also be made as a quiche if you use the pastry recipe from the tart on page 114, but it's lovely and rich with just the cheese and meat, so I prefer it as a frittata. I like to serve this with a Pinot Grigio to balance the richness.

20 g/generous 1 tablespoon butter

8–10 spring onions/scallions, sliced

6 eggs, beaten

2 tablespoons milk

a big pinch of freshly chopped parsley

1 tablespoon crème fraîche/sour cream

60 g/2¼ oz. soft goats' cheese (or soft cheese of your choice)

100 g/3¾ oz. coppa or salami, sliced

sea salt and freshly ground black pepper

salad leaves/greens, to serve

2 lemon quarters, to serve (optional)

SERVES 2

Heat the butter in a frying pan/skillet until melted, then fry the spring onions/scallions over high heat, until soft and browned. Meanwhile, mix the eggs with the milk, parsley and some salt and pepper. Pour the beaten egg mixture over the spring onions/scallions and stir once to mix well. Turn the heat down to medium and leave the egg mixture to cook (without stirring) until it starts to thicken.

Meanwhile, preheat the grill/broiler to high.

Once the bottom of the frittata starts to set in the frying pan/skillet, put the crème fraîche/sour cream on the top of the frittata in evenly spaced 'dollops'. Do the same with the pieces of goats' cheese and then with the slices of coppa, pushing the middle of the slices down slightly so the sides fold up.

Transfer the frying pan/skillet to the preheated grill/broiler and grill/broil for about 5 minutes, until the top browns. Keep checking the frittata regularly to make sure it doesn't burn.

Serve immediately, sliced into wedges. Serve with a side of dressed salad leaves/greens and a lemon quarter to squeeze over the top, if you like.

LARGER DISHES

HOME-MADE PIZZA

What better way to celebrate salumi than by putting it on an Italian pizza with Italian cheese? The look of the pepperoni pizza is often associated with cheap, poor-quality pizzas, but it is so different when you make it yourself and use good-quality ingredients. The ease of this recipe is that only the dough needs any preparation; the other ingredients are already prepared for you.

FOR THE BASE/CRUST

170 g/1½ cups plain/all-purpose or wholemeal/whole-wheat flour

a small pinch of fast-action/rapid-rise yeast

1 tablespoon olive oil

a pinch of sea salt

2 teaspoons caster/granulated sugar

FOR THE TOPPING

400-g/14-oz. can of tomatoes, drained and chopped

1 tablespoon tomato purée/paste

a big pinch of freshly chopped parsley

a big pinch of freshly chopped or dried oregano

about 40 g/1½ oz. Caramelized Red Onions (see page 147) (optional)

150 g/5 oz. mozzarella cheese, torn into pieces

8–10 slices salami or saucisson sec

50 g/2 oz. pecorino cheese, grated or shaved

a few fresh basil leaves

sea salt and freshly ground black pepper

a large baking sheet, greased or lined with parchment paper

MAKES 1 PIZZA

Preheat the oven to 180°C (350°F) Gas 4.

For the base/crust, put all the ingredients in a bowl, add 125 ml/½ cup water and mix together with your hands to make a dough. If the mixture feels sloppy, just add a little more flour, or add a little more water for the opposite (it shouldn't be so dry that it crumbles when you roll it). Turn the dough out onto a flour-dusted surface and knead for 5–10 minutes, until smooth and elastic. The kneading is always a bit boring but just remember that you need (groan!) to do it or your base will be chewy and tough. If you have a bread maker, it will do the work for you – just follow the timing instructions for your machine.

Place the dough back in the bowl and cover with a damp tea towel/kitchen towel for about 1 hour, until risen slightly.

Transfer the dough to a flour-dusted surface and punch it down gently to release the air. Roll out the dough to a large round – we like a thin pizza base/crust but you can keep it thicker, if you prefer. Put the pizza base/crust on the prepared baking sheet and bake in the preheated oven for 10 minutes, turning over halfway through. It really helps to part-bake the base/crust on its own like this first, so that you don't have to bake it for too long with the topping on (and risk the topping burning or shrivelling up).

Meanwhile, prepare the topping. Mix the canned tomatoes, tomato purée/paste, parsley and oregano in a bowl, and season with salt and pepper.

Remove the pizza base/crust from the oven and turn it over so the softer side that was touching the baking sheet is now facing up. Spread the tomato mixture evenly over the top and then spoon over the caramelized onions, if using. Distribute the mozzarella cheese over the tomato mixture, followed by the salami slices, and finally sprinkle over the pecorino cheese. Sprinkle the basil leaves on top.

Return the pizza to the preheated oven on the middle shelf (ideally, put the pizza directly onto the oven shelf, rather than using the baking sheet, so the base/crust can continue to crisp) and bake for a further 15 minutes, until the cheese has melted. Serve hot.

PANCAKE 'CALZONES'

A savoury folded pancake with mortadella, mozzarella (or Gorgonzola) and fried Mediterranean vegetables with pesto. Not usually one to be beaten by any recipe containing meat and cheese, even my husband Roland found this recipe as a traditional calzone (made with pizza dough) a bit rich, and he had the idea of trying it as a savoury pancake, which was much less filling and also brought out the flavours of the mortadella.

FOR THE PANCAKE BATTER

40 g/⅓ cup plain/all-purpose flour

a pinch of sea salt

1 egg, beaten

50 ml/scant ¼ cup milk

20 g/generous 1 tablespoon butter

FOR THE FILLING

1 garlic clove, finely chopped

6–7 button/white mushrooms, sliced

1 courgette/zucchini, thinly sliced

1 tablespoon olive oil

4–5 sun-dried tomatoes, chopped

200-g/7-oz. can of tomatoes, drained

1 tablespoon tomato purée/paste

1 tablespoon pesto

a handful of fresh basil leaves

200 g/7 oz. mortadella, torn into pieces

200 g/7 oz. mozzarella, torn (or use Gorgonzola, crumbled, for a richer feast)

sea salt and freshly ground black pepper

MAKES 2

To make the batter, sift the flour and salt into a bowl, then whisk/beat in the egg, milk and 1 tablespoon cold water to make a smooth batter. Cover and leave in the refrigerator whilst you prepare the filling.

For the filling, fry the garlic, mushrooms and courgette/zucchini with the olive oil in a frying pan/skillet over medium heat, until brown, then add the sun-dried tomatoes, canned tomatoes, tomato purée/paste, pesto and basil leaves, season with salt and pepper, and stir until hot. Remove from the heat and keep hot.

Meanwhile, make the pancakes. Heat another frying pan/skillet over medium heat and melt half the butter. Once the butter is melted, pour half of the batter evenly into the pan, swirling it around to coat the bottom of the pan, and leave to cook.

Once the bottom is cooked, flip the pancake over, then spoon half of the vegetable mixture onto one side of the pancake. Quickly add half of the mortadella and mozzarella, then fold the pancake over and keep it over low heat for 1–2 minutes more, until the cheese has melted. Repeat with the remaining butter, batter and vegetables to make a second calzone. Serve immediately.

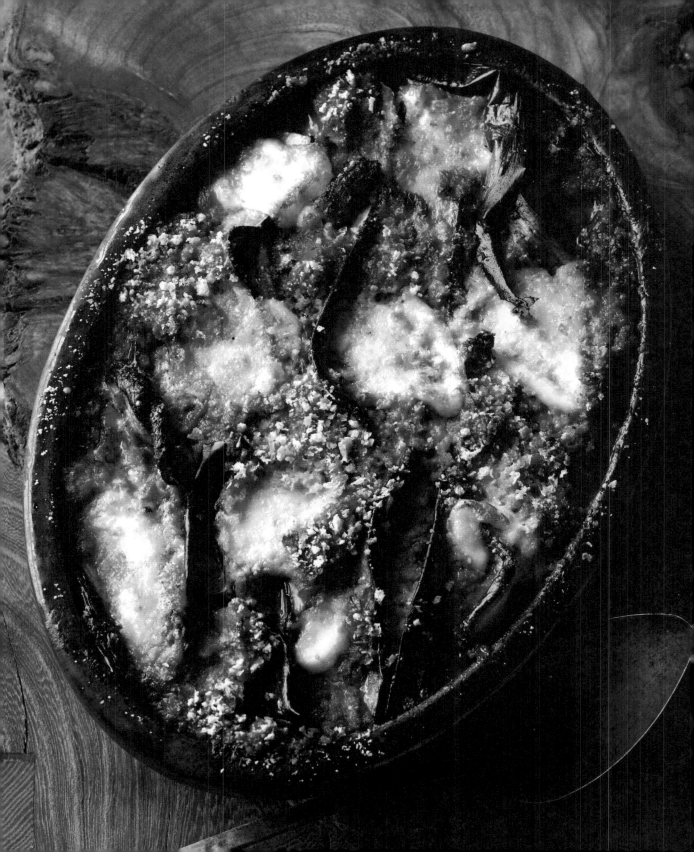

AUBERGINE PARMIGIANA

Now I know this is meant to be a vegetarian dish, but I'm incapable of leaving meat out of a recipe. I just am. If you can make the tomato sauce the day before and chill it in the refrigerator overnight, the flavour is better. Otherwise, once the sauce is made, fill a sink with cold water and lower the base of the frying pan/skillet into the water to cool the sauce. This is a good trick for getting the best flavour from your sauce!

3 aubergines/eggplants, cut into 5-mm/¼-inch slices

1 onion, finely chopped

1 garlic clove, finely chopped

100 g/3¾ oz. pancetta, diced (you can use the Home-cured Pancetta from page 126, if you like)

1 teaspoon tomato purée/paste

freshly chopped or dried oregano

1 teaspoon soft/packed brown sugar

a small pinch of ground nutmeg

1 tablespoon white wine vinegar

2 x 400-g/14-oz. cans of chopped tomatoes

10–12 fresh basil leaves

300 g/11 oz. buffalo mozzarella, drained

1 teaspoon finely grated Parmesan cheese

1 teaspoon breadcrumbs

sea salt and freshly ground black pepper

olive oil, for cooking

large ovenproof dish (about 35 x 25 cm/14 x 10 inches), greased

SERVES 2

Preheat the grill/broiler to high.

Rub olive oil over some foil or onto a baking sheet and set aside. Rub more olive oil over the top of each slice of aubergine/eggplant. Put a single layer of aubergine/eggplant slices on the prepared baking sheet. Grill/broil under the preheated grill/broiler for 4–5 minutes on each side and then remove to a plate. Grill/broil the remaining aubergine/eggplant slices in the same way, cooking them in batches. You can then lay the cooked slices on some paper towels to soak up some of the olive oil, if you want to. Set aside.

Meanwhile, to make the tomato sauce, fry the onion, garlic and pancetta in a frying pan/skillet with a little olive oil until they're all soft and browned. Add the tomato purée/paste, oregano, sugar and nutmeg, and season with salt and pepper. Stir for a minute. Add the vinegar and then add the canned tomatoes. Tear in the basil leaves, then reduce the heat to low and simmer for 10 minutes. Remove from the heat and let cool (see introduction above).

Now you are ready to assemble the dish.

Preheat the oven to 180°C (350°F) Gas 4.

Spread some of the tomato sauce over the base of the prepared ovenproof dish, then lay some of the aubergine/eggplant slices over the top to cover the sauce. Take a third of the mozzarella and tear it into little strips, then sprinkle over the aubergine/eggplant slices.

Spoon over some more tomato sauce and repeat the layer of aubergine/eggplant slices, then another third of the mozzarella. Repeat the layers for a third and final time, finishing with a last bit of tomato sauce dotted about on the top. Mix the Parmesan cheese and breadcrumbs in a bowl, then sprinkle over the top.

Bake in the preheated oven for 25 minutes. If you want to brown the top a little more, pop the dish under a preheated hot grill/broiler for 2–3 minutes so the topping browns off nicely. The mozzarella will be melted and gooey on every layer, and the sauce with the added pancetta is delicious and thick between the aubergine/eggplant slices. Serve immediately.

This is my sister's favourite dish, so I'm going to recommend a glass of sparkling rosé to go with it, because I know she loves that too!

SMOKED SAUSAGE CASSEROLE

A really good-quality smoked sausage is divine. Beware of the cheaper alternatives; they're only exploiting the tradition of mixing the meat with lots of lovely herbs and seasoning and adding the smoked flavour. I'd still recommend looking at the ingredients and the traceability before buying one. This is a recipe to make a rich, warming casserole using smoked sausage – it's easy to make and it freezes well too.

20 g/generous 1 tablespoon butter

1 red onion, chopped

1 garlic clove, chopped

1 red/bell pepper, deseeded and chopped

200 g/7 oz. mushrooms, halved (such as button/white or chestnut mushrooms)

5 tablespoons red wine

20 g/¾ oz. plain/all-purpose flour

400 ml/1⅔ cups chicken stock

1 bay leaf

a sprig of fresh thyme

200 g/7 oz. smoked sausage, chopped

sea salt and freshly ground black pepper

SERVES 2

Melt the butter in a heavy-based saucepan over medium heat, add the onion and garlic and fry for about 5 minutes, until softened. Add the red/bell pepper and mushrooms and cook, stirring, until they soften. Pour in the red wine and let that reduce a little, then sprinkle the flour over the top and stir for a minute or so to mix. Pour over the chicken stock and stir well. Add the herbs and smoked sausage, and season with salt and pepper.

Bring to the boil, then reduce the heat to low. Cover and simmer for 1½ hours. For a thicker casserole, leave the casserole cooking for 2 hours.

Remove and discard the bay leaf and thyme stalk before serving. Serve with mashed potato and a glass of German beer.

Cook's Note
This casserole freezes well for up to 3 months. Defrost thoroughly and then bring gently to the boil before serving – top up the seasoning a bit if you need to as well.

PAELLA

If I wasn't laughed at so much when I asked if 'paella' was Spanish for 'bung it all in a pan and let it go gooey', then I'd still happily believe that to be the case. Paella is so simple, so delicious (to my taste and to many like me), and it's a great way to show off your home curing, if you're doing any from Chapter 5. This makes 2 generous portions.

1 tablespoon olive oil

4 shallots, finely chopped

1 garlic clove, finely chopped

100 g/3¾ oz. skinless, boneless chicken breast or thigh meat, diced

100 g/3¾ oz. chorizo, diced (you can use your Home-made Fresh Chorizo from page 129, but add it later – see Cook's Note)

100 g/3¾ oz. pancetta, diced (you can use your Home-cure Pancetta here too – see page 126)

1 red/bell pepper, deseeded and roughly chopped

a small handful of green beans, trimmed and roughly chopped

200 g/7 oz. shelled uncooked seafood (such as scallops, mussels and sliced squid)

12–14 uncooked king prawns/jumbo shrimp, shelled and deveined

1 small fresh red chilli/chili, deseeded and finely chopped

1 teaspoon paprika

a pinch of chipotle powder (optional)

50 g/½ cup frozen or fresh peas

a small handful of freshly chopped parsley

a pinch of freshly chopped or dried thyme

6 tablespoons white wine (preferably dry)

500 ml/generous 2 cups hot chicken stock

150 g/5 oz. paella rice, such as Bomba

a small pinch of saffron strands

sea salt and freshly ground black pepper

crème fraîche/sour cream and 1 lemon, quartered, to serve (optional)

SERVES 2

Put the olive oil in a frying pan/skillet over medium heat and get it nice and hot, then add the shallots and garlic and cook them until browned. Then, it's a simple process of adding everything as you go through the list. Add the chicken and cook, turning regularly, until sealed. Add the chorizo and stir for 20 seconds, then add the pancetta and cook, stirring, until the pancetta and chorizo are becoming crisp. Add the red/bell pepper, and stir for 20 seconds, then add the green beans and cook for 20 seconds. Add the seafood and prawns, followed by the chilli/chili and spices, and stir to coat everything. Add the peas and herbs, then add the wine and turn the heat up to bubble the wine for 2 minutes. Add the stock, rice and saffron, then season with salt and pepper.

Turn the heat right down so the mixture is just lightly bubbling and cook, stirring occasionally, for 15–20 minutes, until the rice has absorbed all the liquid and all the ingredients are cooked. You'll know if you like it a bit runny, or thicker, so just keep an eye on the consistency and be sure to taste the rice towards the end of cooking so that you know it is definitely cooked. You can always add a little more hot stock if you want the rice 'fluffier' and then just cook for a bit longer.

Once the paella is ready, serve it immediately with the crème fraîche/sour cream and lemon quarters.

Cook's Note

If you're using your Home-made Fresh Chorizo (see page 129), I would add it later, just before the white wine and chicken stock. Stir it carefully so as not to break up the chorizo (remember it hasn't got a skin), but the breadcrumbs in it will help to hold it together. It will continue to cook while you're simmering the rice and will contribute to the lovely, salty paprika flavours.

GRILLED HALVED CHORIZO WITH PAPRIKA AND PARMESAN MASH

This is a charcuterie version of the traditional 'sausage and mash' meal. It's richer, with the chorizo and the flavoured mash, so that's why I would recommend mixing potato mash with squash mash to lighten it. If you normally eat three sausages, you'll probably only need three halved chorizo pieces, rather than six (that means you, Roland…).

½ butternut squash, peeled, deseeded and chopped

2 baking potatoes, chopped

15–20-cm/6–8-inch length of whole chorizo, cut into 5-cm/2-inch lengths

10 g/2 teaspoons butter

3 tablespoons milk

1 teaspoon paprika

a pinch of chipotle powder

30 g/1¼ oz. Parmesan cheese, grated

sea salt and freshly ground black pepper

snipped fresh chives or parsley, to garnish

SERVES 2

Put the squash and potatoes in a saucepan, cover with cold water, bring to the boil and boil for 15–20 minutes, until cooked.

Meanwhile, preheat the grill/broiler to high.

Slice the chorizo pieces lengthways in half and peel off the casing. Pop the chorizo pieces under the grill/broiler for 10 minutes, turning once. A good chorizo shouldn't shrivel too much, but just keep an eye on it. Remove from the heat.

Drain the squash and potatoes, return to the pan and mash well with the butter and milk. Add the paprika, chipotle powder and Parmesan cheese, and season with salt and pepper. Stir well.

Serve the mash with the grilled/broiled chorizo and garnish with some snips of fresh chives or parsley on top. This dish goes well with Sweet Chilli Sticky Sweetcorn (see page 142).

Cook's Note
You can also cook the Home-made Fresh Chorizo recipe on page 129 to serve with the mash.

SPAGHETTI CARBONARA

This is a great dish to make to show off your Home-cured Pancetta or Bacon (see page 126–127), or just use shop-bought pancetta, if you prefer. If you're using Home-cured Pancetta or Bacon, I recommend blanching it in a pan of boiling water for 2 minutes to decrease the saltiness, then drain, before frying it as directed in the recipe below.

200 g/7 oz. dried spaghetti or linguine

50 g/3½ tablespoons butter

2 garlic cloves, finely chopped

200 g/7 oz. pancetta or streaky/fatty bacon, cut into small cubes

2 eggs, beaten

75 g/scant ½ cup finely grated Parmesan cheese

a big pinch of freshly chopped parsley

1 tablespoon crème fraîche/sour cream

sea salt and freshly ground black pepper

SERVES 2

First, cook the spaghetti in a pan of lightly salted boiling water until it is cooked to your liking. Once the spaghetti is cooked, drain it, reserving 5-mm/¼-inch of the cooking water in the base of the pan, and keep this over low heat.

Meanwhile, melt the butter in a frying pan/skillet over medium heat and fry the garlic until soft. Add the pancetta and fry until crispy and browned. Remove from the heat and keep warm in the pan.

In a large bowl, beat the eggs and then mix in most of the Parmesan cheese, reserving just a little cheese to sprinkle on the top. Add the parsley and crème fraîche/sour cream and a good crunch of black pepper. Set aside.

Add the drained hot spaghetti to the beaten egg mixture and mix a little, then return the spaghetti and egg mixture to the pan containing the reserved pasta cooking water and stir. You don't want the egg mixture to scramble, but let it mix with the hot pasta water to create a sauce. Stir in the crispy pancetta and garlic mixture.

Serve immediately with the remaining Parmesan cheese sprinkled on top, and a crunch more pepper or a little more freshly chopped parsley, as you wish.

SCRAMBLED EGG, ROASTED VINE TOMATOES AND PROSCIUTTO WITH PORCINI MUSHROOM PURÉE

When you take some of the components of a traditional 'English Breakfast' and prepare it like this, you can eat it for any meal in the day, I reckon.

15 g/½ oz. dried porcini mushrooms (or 25 g/1 oz. fresh porcini mushrooms, finely chopped)

8 tomatoes on the vine

2 tablespoons olive oil

25 g/2 tablespoons butter, plus 10 g/¼ oz.

1 garlic clove

1 tablespoon crème fraîche/sour cream

a big pinch of freshly snipped chives

4 eggs

50 ml/scant ¼ cup whole milk

6 slices prosciutto

sea salt and freshly ground black pepper

Serves 2

Preheat the oven to 190°C (375°F) Gas 5.

First, start the porcini mushroom purée. If you're using dried porcini mushrooms, as I usually do, soak them in boiling water for about 20 minutes, then drain and finely chop.

While the mushrooms are soaking, prepare the roasted tomatoes.

Keep the tomatoes on the vine and put them in an ovenproof dish, then drizzle over the olive oil. Season with salt and pepper. Roast in the preheated oven for 20–25 minutes, until they start to brown and are soft.

Meanwhile, finish making the porcini purée. Melt the 10 g/¼ oz. butter in a frying pan/skillet, then add the garlic and soaked or fresh porcini mushrooms. Mix in the crème fraîche/sour cream and stir well. Remove from the heat and keep hot. Serve with the snipped chives sprinkled on the top.

A few minutes before you are ready to serve, make the scrambled eggs. In a bowl, beat the eggs, milk and a bit of pepper together really well. Melt the remaining 25 g/2 tablespoons butter in a separate frying pan/skillet and pour in the egg mixture, stirring constantly to keep it from setting or sticking. Continue cooking and stirring, until the eggs are scrambled to your liking.

Serve the prosciutto slices as they are, or, in the pan that you used for the porcini mushroom purée, lay the slices in there and cook for just a couple of minutes on each side, turning once, so that they start to crisp and soak up some of the flavour of the mushrooms.

Serve the scrambled eggs with the porcini purée, roasted tomatoes and prosciutto slices.

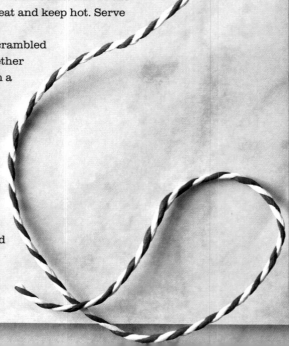

CRISP FRIED MONKFISH WITH PANCETTA AND CAPERS

This recipe is easy but it needs to be made just before serving, so it's not ideal for a dinner party as it will tie you up in the kitchen – even though the smells wafting from there will whet their appetites marvellously. It does look jolly snazzy though, so be sure to brag about it with a photo.

300 g/10 oz. monkfish fillets, sliced into strips

30 g/¼ cup plain/all-purpose flour

2 eggs, beaten

30 g/1½ cup fresh breadcrumbs

2 tablespoons olive oil

200 g/7 oz cubed pancetta

2 tablespoons small capers, drained

freshly grated zest of ½ lemon

1 teaspoon freshly chopped parsley

½ lemon, cut into quarters

2 Salumi Chips (see page 142) (optional)

sea salt and freshly ground black pepper

Asparagus and Prosciutto Gratin (see page 139), to serve

SERVES 2

Roll the strips of monkfish in the flour to coat all over, then dip each strip into the beaten eggs and finally coat with breadcrumbs. Reserve any leftover breadcrumbs.

Heat the olive oil in a large frying pan/skillet over medium heat. Add the pancetta and fry until crisp, then remove from the pan and set aside. Place the coated fish strips into the pan and cook for 6–7 minutes without turning, then turn them carefully and fry for a further 6–7 minutes on the other side, until crisp and cooked through. While they're frying, sprinkle the capers, lemon zest and parsley over the top so that they fry with the monkfish and pick up the oil and flavours in the pan. You can sprinkle any leftover breadcrumbs over at this stage too, if you like, so that they add a bit of crunch to the capers. Add the pancetta back into the pan when the fish is almost cooked.

Once the fish strips are cooked and crisp, remove from the heat. Serve on plates with the capers and pancetta from the pan, and some lemon wedges on the side. Serve with the Asparagus and Prosciutto Gratin. Top each portion with a baked salumi chip, if you like – either by placing them on the top or crunching them into little shards to sprinkle over the top.

Cook's Note
This is delicious served with a home-made sweet chilli sauce. Heat 40 g/3 tablespoons butter in a frying pan/skillet until melted, add 2 finely chopped deseeded/seeded chillies/chiles, stir well then add 2 tablespoons white wine vinegar and 6 tablespoons demerara/raw sugar, stirring together well. Let the mixture boil and start to thicken, then slowly add 100 ml/⅓ cup water, stirring well. Remove from the heat and let cool, either in the refrigerator or by lowering the pan into a sinkful of cold water to cool the sauce quickly.

CHORIZO, SPRING ONION AND MANGO NOODLES

I don't think there's any reason to be nervous about mixing up the geography of food; salumi can be delicious in East Asian dishes. It's a bit like this recipe, with sweetness in the mango, a kick from the chilli/chile, and then the flavours of the diced chorizo or, if you can get it, soppressata, another lovely, rich cured pork product.

1 tablespoon sesame oil

8 spring onions/scallions, chopped

1 garlic clove, finely chopped

200 g/7 oz. chorizo, diced (or use soppressata)

a pinch of ground ginger (or use grated peeled fresh root ginger)

1 small fresh red chilli/chile, deseeded/seeded and chopped

1 pak choi/bok choy, chopped

1 teaspoon soft/packed brown sugar

2 tablespoons soy sauce

a big pinch of freshly chopped coriander/cilantro

½ mango, peeled, stoned/pitted and chopped

250 g/8 oz. noodles (see Cook's Note)

sea salt and freshly ground black pepper

SERVES 2

Heat the sesame oil in a frying pan/skillet or wok and fry the spring onions/scallions and garlic over medium-high heat, until soft and brown. Add the chorizo, ginger, red chilli/chile and pak choi/bok choy, and season with salt and pepper, then cook, stirring for a minute or two, until the pak choi/bok choy starts to soften. Add the sugar, soy sauce and coriander/cilantro, and stir well. Add the mango on top for the last few minutes of cooking.

Meanwhile, cook the noodles as instructed on the packet. Drain well.

Add the cooked noodles to the stir-fried mixture and toss to mix. Serve immediately, or cool, chill and eat it cold the next day.

Cook's Note

This dish is particularly good made with rice noodles, as the chorizo gives a richer flavour than is usual in this type of dish.

SCALLOP, CHORIZO, CHILLI AND QUINOA STEW WITH HERBY DUMPLINGS

So many cured meats come from warm Southern European plains where there's a sea breeze and sunshine on the roofs... However, this is a stew recipe that's perfect for when it's chilly outside and you need some central heating for the tummy. The chorizo and the chilli/chile provide the most amazing warmth with their flavour.

FOR THE STEW

20 g/generous 1 tablespoon butter

1 red onion, diced

1 garlic clove, chopped

1 red/bell pepper, deseeded and diced

2 celery stalks, chopped

100 g/3¾ oz. chorizo, diced

1 small fresh red chilli/chile, deseeded and finely chopped

1 teaspoon paprika

30 g/scant ⅓ cup plain/all-purpose flour

500 ml/generous 2 cups chicken stock

100 g/3¾ oz. quinoa or pearl barley

200 g/7 oz. shelled scallops

sea salt and freshly ground black pepper

FOR THE HERBY DUMPLINGS (OPTIONAL)

50 g/⅓ cup shredded suet

100 g/¾ cup self-raising/self-rising flour

a pinch of dried thyme

a pinch of dried rosemary

a baking sheet, greased

SERVES 2

For the stew, melt the butter in a frying pan/skillet, then fry the onion and garlic over low heat for 10 minutes, until softened. Add the red/bell pepper and celery, and fry until the vegetables soften. Add the chorizo, red chilli/chile and paprika, and season with salt and pepper, then stir to mix. Sprinkle the flour over the top and stir for just a minute before adding the chicken stock. Stir in the quinoa.

Bring to a simmer and simmer for 35 minutes, stirring occasionally, then add the scallops. Cook for a further 10 minutes (or 15 minutes if the scallops are frozen), until the scallops are cooked.

If you would like to make the herby dumplings, start making them as soon as the stew begins simmering.

Preheat the oven to 180°C (350°F) Gas 4.

Put all the dumpling ingredients in a bowl and stir to mix, then gradually add 50–100 ml/scant ¼–⅓ cup cold water, a little at a time, and keep mixing with your hands until the mixture comes together in a solid ball. Don't make the mixture too wet, otherwise the dumplings will be soggy.

Divide and roll the mixture into round dumplings and put them onto the prepared baking sheet. Bake in the preheated oven for 15 minutes, then add them to the stew for the last 25 minutes of cooking time. Serve hot.

MEDITERRANEAN PASTA BAKE WITH CRISPY BAKED SALUMI

This is a good one for entertaining because you can prepare and throw everything together earlier in the day, then all you have to do is bake the dish and add the crispy salumi in the last 10 minutes. It looks like more effort than it is as well.

FOR THE PASTA BAKE

1 tablespoon olive oil

1 red onion, finely chopped

2 garlic cloves, finely chopped

1 courgette/zucchini, chopped

1 aubergine/eggplant, chopped

1 red/bell pepper, deseeded/seeded and chopped

8–10 button/white mushrooms, chopped

2 tablespoons tomato purée/paste

1 tablespoon pesto

2 x 400-g/7-oz. cans of chopped tomatoes

8 handfuls of dried pasta

250 ml/1 cup crème fraîche/sour cream

200 g/7 oz. mozzarella, torn into pieces

4 Salumi Chips (see page 142)

sea salt and freshly ground black pepper

SERVES 4

For the pasta bake, heat the olive oil in a frying pan/skillet over medium heat until hot, then add the onion, garlic, courgette/zucchini, aubergine/eggplant, red/bell pepper and mushrooms, and fry until they're all soft and browning. Add the tomato purée/paste and pesto, season with salt and pepper, and stir together for a minute, then add the canned tomatoes. Reduce the heat and simmer for 10 minutes.

Meanwhile, cook the pasta in a large pan of lightly salted boiling water for 3 minutes (it's only to soften it), then drain well and return to the pan. Add the vegetable mixture and stir well, then stir in the crème fraîche/sour cream. Taste and add more seasoning, if you like. Transfer the mixture to an ovenproof dish and spread evenly. At this point, you can cover the dish with foil and leave it for a while before baking, or cool it, then chill in the refrigerator for up to 2 days.

When you are ready to serve, preheat the oven to 180°C (350°F) Gas 4.

Dot the mozzarella over the top of the pasta mixture, then cover with foil and bake in the preheated oven for 30 minutes. After around 25 minutes, remove the aluminium foil to brown the top (alternatively, pop the pasta bake under a preheated hot grill/broiler for the last 5 minutes to brown the top).

Serve the pasta bake with the crispy salumi alongside, on top or on the side.

SLOW-COOKED, DRY-RUB PORK RIBS WITH BBQ SAUCE

The process of curing and preserving also taught us a lot about flavour. Dry rubs, for example, are short cures designed more for flavour than shelf-life, but they still follow the same process of rubbing the seasoning into the outside of meat so that it can soak up the salt and flavours. You'll need to start this the day before you want to serve it.

1 pork rack, about 5 or 6 bones (about 1.5 kg/3½ lbs.), trimmed

2 tablespoons sea salt

2 tablespoons dark soft/packed brown sugar

2 teaspoons paprika

½ teaspoon cayenne pepper

3 tablespoons brandy

Chunky BBQ Sauce, to serve (see page 150)

SERVES 4

Remove the fat along the top of the pork rack using a sharp knife, and set the fat aside. Mix the salt, sugar, paprika and cayenne pepper together in a bowl and then rub most of this mixture all over the joint – be sure to get in-between the trimmed bones. Place the reserved layer of fat back on top of the rack, then rub the remaining seasoning mixture over the top of that too. Wrap the joint in clingfilm/plastic wrap and leave in the refrigerator overnight or for at least 3 hours.

Preheat the oven to 200°C (400°F) Gas 6.

Unwrap the joint and put it in an ovenproof dish or roasting pan. Drizzle the brandy over the top. Roast in the preheated oven for 25–30 minutes, so the outside just begins to brown. Reduce the oven temperature down to 120°C (250°F) Gas ½. Remove the dish or pan from the oven and transfer the joint onto some foil (I recommend doubling the foil so it's stronger). Wrap the foil over the top of the joint, enclosing the meat, then return it to the dish or pan. Pour in some water around the edge so that it's about 2-cm/¾-inch high in the dish. Return to the oven and cook for a further 3 hours.

Remove from the oven. Carefully open the foil and use a fork to test the meat – put the fork into the side of the joint and twist; if the meat is still solid and doesn't shred at all, it needs longer in the oven. Return it to the oven and check again after 30 minutes. When it's ready, the joint won't fall apart at the sides, but you should be able to turn the fork and see the pork meat start to shred.

Turn the oven back up to 200°C (400°F) Gas 6.

Undo the aluminium foil and remove the layer of fat from the top of the joint (you can make crackling with this, if you like), then, with the aluminium foil still open to expose the joint, return it to the hot oven for 20 minutes, until the top is crisp.

Remove from the oven. You can then slice the joint between the bones and serve it as chops or strip the meat off the bone, pull/shred it, then serve in a roll with the Chunky BBQ Sauce

TARTE AU SAUCISSON SEC WITH CARAMELISED RED ONION, BRIE AND TARRAGON PASTRY

This was the first recipe I tried for this book! It was a regular Tuesday evening and Roland said, 'What's for supper?' When I replied with this title, he realized that supper was going to be a lot of fun for a couple of months. He also realized that he might have to plan to go to the gym a little more too. (NB I know ours was a rather gender-stereotyped exchange about supper, but even when Roland insists on doing the cooking, it starts with a bit of fussing on my part and ends in a coup d'état, so he finds jobs elsewhere...!).

1 red onion, thinly sliced

2 tablespoons runny honey

100 g/3½ oz. butter (at room temperature)

220 g/1¾ cups plain/all-purpose flour

a big pinch of sea salt

a big pinch of dried tarragon

200 g/7 oz. Brie, sliced

7–8 slices saucisson sec (about 60 g/2¼ oz.)

100 ml/⅓ cup crème fraîche/sour cream

freshly ground black pepper

dressed salad leaves/greens, to serve

tart pan or baking sheet, greased

SERVES 2

Preheat the oven to 180°C (350°F) Gas 4.

Put the onion in an ovenproof dish, drizzle over the honey and stir to mix. Roast in the preheated oven for 15 minutes, until caramelized.

Meanwhile, to make the pastry base, rub the butter and flour together in a bowl with your fingers until crumbly, then add the salt and tarragon. Add about 1 tablespoon cold water and mix to make a dough, but don't let the mixture get too soggy. Gather the pastry into a ball, then turn it out onto a flour-dusted surface and roll out.

Use the rolling pin to help you transfer the pastry to the prepared tart pan and gently press it into the base and up the sides of the pan (or transfer the pastry to a greased baking sheet if you don't have a suitable tart pan – just make sure you fold in the edges so the topping doesn't leak out during cooking).

Prick the base of the pastry all over with a fork, then bake the pastry base on its own in the preheated oven for 5 minutes. Arrange the brie slices over the pastry base, then sprinkle the caramelized onions over the top. Put the slices of saucisson sec over the onions, then add little blobs of crème fraîche/sour cream around the top. Add a sprinkling of pepper.

Bake in the preheated oven for a further 20–25 minutes.

Serve with dressed salad leaves/greens and an ice-cold glass of wine or cider.

LEFTOVER ROAST HAM OMELETTE

The simple omelette/omelet is one of my favourite ways to use up leftover cold roast ham. Even the shredded bits left on the board are perfect for the omelette mixture.

6 eggs

a good splash of milk, about 25 ml/1½ tablespoons

1 tablespoon freshly chopped parsley

a small pinch of mustard powder

a handful of leftover cold cooked ham, chopped or shredded

a handful of mature Cheddar cheese, cubed (optional)

20 g/generous 1 tablespoon butter

sea salt and freshly ground black pepper

SERVES 2

Crack the eggs into a bowl and beat them really well, then add the milk, parsley and mustard powder, season with salt and pepper, and mix well. Throw in the ham and cubes of Cheddar, if using.

Heat the butter in a frying pan/skillet over fairly high heat until it's fully melted and the pan is very hot. Pour in the egg mixture, pushing any away from the sides of the pan. Turn the heat right down and let the omelette/omelet cook slowly.

Once the bottom half of the omelette/omelet is solid, you can use a heatproof spatula to flip one side over. Cook until the eggs are set. Alternatively, leave the omelette/omelet flat and finish it under a hot grill/broiler.

Once the omelette/omelet is cooked, serve it immediately.

Cook's Note

If you want a slightly more filling meal, this is great served with 'Sweet Patatas Bravas' (see page 140), as the tomato sauce is as lovely with the omelette/omelet as it is with the roasted sweet potatoes.

CHICKEN BREAST WRAPPED IN PROSCIUTTO WITH GRIDDLED CHICORY

This makes an impressive dinner party dish and works brilliantly with Chorizo and Red Cabbage Salad (see page 79).

1 tablespoon red wine vinegar

1 tablespoon olive oil, plus extra for griddling

1 teaspoon soft/packed brown sugar

1 garlic clove, finely chopped

a big pinch of freshly chopped parsley

a pinch each of sea salt and freshly ground black pepper

2 skinless, boneless chicken breasts

4 slices prosciutto

1 chicory/Belgian endive, halved

1 teaspoon paprika

Chorizo and Red Cabbage Salad, to serve (see page 79)

SERVES 2

Put the vinegar, olive oil, sugar, garlic, parsley and salt and pepper in a bowl and mix together, then rub this mixture into the chicken breasts. Wrap the chicken in clingfilm/plastic wrap and leave in the refrigerator for at least 1 hour.

Remove from the refrigerator, then wrap each chicken breast in 2 slices of prosciutto.

Heat a ridged stove-top griddle/grill pan over a high heat with a drop more olive oil added to the pan, then add the prosciutto-wrapped chicken breasts to the hot pan and cook for 6–7 minutes. Place the chicory/Belgian endive halves, flat-sides down, next to the chicken in the same pan. Turn the wrapped breasts and leave to cook on the other side, until cooked through. Sprinkle the paprika over the top of the wrapped breasts and the chicory/Belgian endive.

Turn the wrapped breasts again before the end of the cooking time and you should have the nice brown griddle lines across the prosciutto. Turn the chicory/Belgian endive halves over near the end of cooking time, just to soften the outside, but they're happy staying face-down for most of the cooking time to get the nice crunchy griddle lines across them as well.

Serve with Chorizo and Red Cabbage Salad.

WURST MEATBALLS

Germany developed the 'wurst' process for curing sausages, but many would argue that it's the best... (pause for laughter!). In the past, Germany excelled at smoking meat and they still make excellent sausages today. As I mentioned in the Introduction, the science is the same, namely to get rid of all the bacteria. Without a smoker at home, nor sausage casing, it's not easy to recreate them, but here's a recipe that uses the ingredients and flavours used for raw 'rohwurst' sausage and it makes lovely meatballs.

200 g/7 oz. minced/ground pork

a pinch of ground mace

a pinch of ground ginger

a pinch of ground nutmeg

a pinch each of sea salt and freshly ground black pepper

½ egg, beaten

1 teaspoon dried milk powder

2 teaspoons breadcrumbs

SERVES 2

Put all the ingredients into a bowl and mix them together really well with your hands. Divide and shape the mixture into 8 even meatballs.

To cook the meatballs, either fry them in a frying pan/skillet over high heat or cook them under a preheated high grill/broiler for 12–15 minutes, turning occasionally.

Once cooked, combine the meatballs with a sauce of your choice and serve with cooked pasta or potatoes, as you wish.

Cook's Note
These meatballs can be used instead of the smoked sausage in the recipe for Smoked Sausage Casserole (see page 94). Just cook the mixture without the meatballs for the first hour, then sear/brown the meatballs separately in a frying pan/skillet for a couple of minutes (or under a preheated hot grill/broiler) so that they hold together well. Add them to the casserole liquid for the last 30–60 minutes so that they combine with the flavours in the pan.

CURED PORK KEBAB SKEWERS

We so often enjoy cured pork loin, we just tend to call it 'bacon'. Here's a good way to use a small joint of cured pork loin to make kebab/kabob skewers with masses of flavour. You'll need to start this the day before you want to serve it.

500 g/1¼ lbs. cured pork loin (smoked or unsmoked)

2 shallots, chopped

1 teaspoon paprika

a pinch of chipotle powder

2 tablespoons sherry

1 teaspoon soft/packed brown sugar

a pinch of freshly chopped or dried parsley

a pinch each of sea salt and freshly ground black pepper

1 courgette/zucchini, sliced

1 fresh Romano chilli/chile, deseeded and sliced

1 tablespoon olive oil

Sweet and Feisty Crème Fraîche, to serve (see page 150)

SERVES 2

The day before you want to serve this, trim the pork loin to remove any rind and reduce the amount of fat on the top as much as you like. Cut the pork into large cubes, about 2-cm/¾-inch in size. Set aside.

Put the shallots, paprika, chipotle powder, sherry, sugar, parsley, and salt and pepper into a food processor and whizz together until well mixed. Transfer the mixture to a polythene food or freezer bag, add the pork pieces and toss to coat them all over with the marinade. Seal the bag and refrigerate overnight to marinate.

The next day, thread the marinated pork pieces and the courgette /zucchini and Romano chilli/chile slices onto metal (or soaked wooden) skewers, alternating the ingredients and dividing them evenly between the skewers.

Heat a ridged stove-top griddle/grill pan over a high heat with the olive oil added to the pan, or preheat a BBQ. Cook the kebabs/kabobs in the pan or over the BBQ, turning them carefully to brown evenly.

Serve with the Sweet and Feisty Crème Fraîche. This is also nice with Sweet Chilli Sticky Sweetcorn (see page 142) and Home-made Chipotle Ketchup (see page 151).

HOME
CURING

HOME-CURED PANCETTA

If you're new to home curing, I really recommend starting with pancetta. The reason for this is that – as well as it being delicious – it's pretty straightforward and there's less margin for error when you're planning to finish the process with a quick fry in a pan as well. It'll build up your confidence and still looks very impressive when you cut it out of the muslin you've had hanging in your fridge for a couple of weeks.

300 g/10 oz. pork belly

2 tablespoons sea salt

1 tablespoon soft/packed brown sugar

1 teaspoon ground garlic powder

1 teaspoon ground black pepper

1 teaspoon dried juniper berries, crushed

1 teaspoon ground coriander (or crushed coriander seeds)

1 teaspoon dried cinnamon

a pinch of mace

sealable container
muslin/cheesecloth
kitchen string/twine

MAKES ABOUT 250 G/8 OZ.

Trim off and discard the rind from the pork belly, then place it in a bowl and add all the other ingredients. Rub the spices all over the surface with your fingers so that the mixture gets into every part of the meat.

Transfer the meat and salt mixture to the container, making sure that the salt mixture covers the bottom of the container and the meat sits on top.

Seal the container and place in the refrigerator for 3 days. Every day, take it out and drain the liquid that is drawn out of the meat. Turn it over at the same time.

After 3 days, remove the meat, wash it under the tap, dry with kitchen paper and then wrap in muslin/cheesecloth and secure with string/twine.

Hang in your fridge for at least 10 days. Check it at 9 or 10 days as it might need a few days longer. Don't worry about leaving it longer, it won't deteriorate for a few weeks and, as you're going to fry it, don't worry about it still being a little pink in the middle either.

When you're ready to cook it, remove from the muslin and dice it into small pieces.

Fry a taster piece first to check the saltiness. If you find it too salty, just boil a pan of water and drop your chopped pieces of pancetta in to blanch for one minute. Drain the water and fry immediately until brown and crispy.

BASIC HOME-CURED BACON

This recipe makes streaky/fatty bacon, and you will really taste the difference from the rashers/strips you buy in the supermarket. You can also use pork loin to make traditional bacon rashers/strips, if you prefer.

400 g/13 oz. pork belly

2 tablespoons sea salt

2 tablespoons soft/packed brown sugar

sealable container
muslin/cheesecloth
kitchen string/twine

MAKES ABOUT 10 RASHERS/STRIPS

Trim off and discard the rind from the pork belly.

Mix the salt and sugar in a bowl and rub all over the pork belly, making sure that it coats every bit of meat.

Transfer the meat and salt mixture to the container, making sure that the salt mixture covers the bottom of the container and the meat sits on top.

Seal the container and place it in the refrigerator for 24 hours.

Drain the liquid that has gathered in the bottom and turn the cut over. Sprinkle a little more salt into the base of the container to keep it off the surface if you need to.

Return it to the fridge for a further 24 hours.

Remove the meat – it will have reduced in size and hardened – rinse it under running water, pat it dry with paper towels, wrap it in a square of muslin/cheesecloth and secure with string/twine. Tie the top of the muslin and hang it in your fridge. Be careful to keep it hanging away from the sides of the fridge or anything else in there.

Tie a tag with the name of the cure (if you're doing more than one) and the date you put it in there or, even easier, the day you need to take it out. Leave it there for 8–10 days.

Remove from the muslin/cheesecloth and slice lengthways to make rashers/strips and then fry or grill/broil, as you choose.

Leave yourself enough time to cook a sample piece, because you'll need to check the saltiness. Either fry or grill a slice and taste. It may well be too salty for your liking, in which case, just boil a pan of water and drop the rest of your slices in to blanch for a minute before cooking. This will draw the salt out and also help to make your bacon really crispy.

HOME-MADE FRESH CHORIZO

The curing process isn't the easiest but the flavour of chorizo is totally delicious and very easy to recreate in fresh sausages. You don't even need sausage casing for this recipe. Make this the day before you plan to cook it, to allow the seasoning to mingle with the pork.

400 g/13 oz. minced/ground pork

1 clove garlic, finely chopped

2 heaped teaspoons ground paprika

a big pinch of dried chilli/hot pepper flakes

a big pinch of dried chipotle powder

a big pinch of dried oregano

sea salt and freshly ground black or pink pepper

6 slices prosciutto

MAKES 6

Put the minced/ground pork, garlic, paprika, dried chilli/hot pepper flakes, dried chipotle powder and oregano into a bowl, and season with salt and pepper. Mix really well with your hands to combine.

Divide the mixture evenly into six portions and roll them into sausage shapes with your hands.

Wrap the sausages in clingfilm/plastic wrap and place in the refrigerator overnight.

When you are ready to serve them, preheat the oven to 180°C (350°F) Gas 4.

Wrap a slice of prosciutto around the outside of each sausage, so it keeps the moisture and oils in during cooking.

Cook in the pre-heated oven for 25 minutes, turning occasionally, until cooked through.

Great served with 'Sweet Patatas Bravas' (see page 140) and an ice-cold beer!

HOME-CURED DUCK BREAST

This is sometimes called 'Duck Ham' or 'Duck Prosciutto', because of the curing process (it doesn't contain any pork). You can do a salt cure but I do recommend adding the sugar because duck has such a rich flavour. Like the home-cured bacons, you can do the salt test before eating.

1 duck breast

3 tablespoons sea salt

2 tablespoons soft/packed brown sugar

1 teaspoon freshly ground black pepper

SERVES 2

Wash the duck breast and dry thoroughly with paper towels. Place the duck in the container and add the other ingredients. Mix well, rubbing the mixture into the duck breast. Make sure there is enough salt and sugar underneath to keep the duck breast off the bottom of the container.

Put the lid on and place in the refrigerator for 24 hours.

Open the lid and drain away the liquid (you'll be amazed how much the salt draws out) and return to the refrigerator for 24 hours more.

Take the duck out of the container, wash it under running water, and dry thoroughly with paper towels. Wrap it in muslin/cheesecloth and tie it securely with kitchen string/twine. Place in the refrigerator for 8–10 days.

Cut a slice off and either taste it uncooked or fry it in a pan. If it tastes too salty for you, you can blanch the slices of breast for 1 minute in boiling water to reduce the intensity of the salt taste.

To serve, fry it or grill/broil it or serve it as it comes on a salad or on bruschetta or crostini. Food safety is vital when serving uncooked cured meats (see the note on page 4).

ROASTING CURED HAM

Cooked ham is delicious for serving hot as a roast and the cold leftovers can be used in many wonderful recipes, like the Leftover Roast Ham Omelette on page 117. This is a guide for cooking a piece of cured gammon about 1–1.5 kg/2–3lb in weight. It's not as simple a science as doubling the instructions for double the weight, but that's a pretty good start for the most part. I do recommend using a temperature probe to get the final, important, part of the roasting right.

4 sticks of celery, roughly chopped

2 onions, roughly chopped

3 carrots, roughly chopped

2 cloves garlic, roughly chopped

2 bay leaves

2 sprigs thyme

1–1.5-kg/2–3-lb boned ham or gammon joint

a small handful of dried juniper berries or pink peppercorns

freshly ground black pepper

SERVES 6–8

Place the celery, onions, carrots, garlic, bay leaves and thyme springs in a large saucepan or pot and add plenty of black pepper. Put the ham joint on top and pour in enough cold water to cover.

Bring to the boil and boil for 20 minutes, then turn off the heat. Let it cool down, with the lid off, for a couple of hours. Place in the refrigerator overnight or for at least 6–7 hours.

Pre-heat the oven to 160°C (350°F) Gas 4.

Remove and discard the string and the rind from the joint; you will probably be able to do this with your hands now that you've soaked it, but use a knife if you need to. Make sure you leave a coating of fat on the top of the meat; don't strip it right down to the meat.

Put the joint into a roasting pan. Use a knife to score the top of the fat into diamond shapes. Push some dried juniper berries or pink peppercorns into the gaps in the fat and crack some black pepper over the top.

Cover the roasting pan with foil, place in the preheated oven and bake for 45 minutes.

Remove the foil and increase the oven temperature to 200°C (400°F) Gas 6.

Return the roasting pan to the oven for 20 minutes, until golden. This is where a thermometer can be a great help, because the outside of a ham always looks 'done' very quickly but you want to make sure the middle of the ham is at least 80°C/175°F on a meat thermometer. Roast for a little longer if it isn't up to temperature yet.

Remove from the oven, cover with foil again and allow the ham to rest for 10 minutes before carving.

To store any unused ham, wrap it in baking parchment and keep in the refrigerator. Clingfilm/plastic wrap or foil tend to make it a bit soggy. Also, we like to tear a bit off every time we walk by the fridge, so wrapping it in paper makes it easier to access! Eat within 1 week.

There's no doubt in my mind that roast ham joints on the bone are more succulent, tasty and tender, but suppliers do a fantastic job now of deboning ham joints, which makes them easier for the home cook.

HONEY AND MUSTARD ROAST HAM

This is a really easy addition to the recipe for the Classic Roast Ham. It's the same process (though I don't use bay leaves for the soaking part).

4 sticks of celery, roughly chopped

2 onions, roughly chopped

3 carrots, roughly chopped

2 cloves garlic, roughly chopped

2 sprigs thyme

1–1.5-kg/2–3-lb boned ham or gammon joint

15 g/1 tablespoon butter

200 ml/generous ¾ cup runny honey

2 teaspoons mustard powder

1 tablespoon wholegrain mustard (or use English or Dijon mustard, if you prefer)

freshly ground black pepper

SERVES 6-8

Place the celery, onions, carrots, garlic and thyme springs in a large saucepan or pot and add plenty of black pepper. Put the ham joint on top and pour in enough cold water to cover.

Bring to the boil and boil for 20 minutes, then turn off the heat. Let it cool down, with the lid off, for a couple of hours. Place in the refrigerator overnight or for at least 6–7 hours.

Pre-heat the oven to 160°C (350°F) Gas 4.

Remove and discard the string and the rind from the joint; you will probably be able to do this with your hands now that you've soaked it, but use a knife if you need to. Make sure you leave a coating of fat on the top of the meat; don't strip it right down to the meat.

Run the butter over the base of a roasting pan, drizzle half of the runny honey over the top and sprinkle over the mustard powder (when this mixture melts, it forms a lovely 'goo' in the base of the dish that we can use to coat the ham). Place the joint on top of the mixture, cover the roasting pan with foil, and bake in the preheated oven for 45 minutes.

Remove the foil and increase the oven temperature to 200°C (400°F) Gas 6.

Roll the joint around in the 'goo' in the bottom of the dish. Squeeze the rest of the runny honey over the top of the joint. Spread the wholegrain mustard over the surface of the ham.

Return the roasting pan to the oven for 20 minutes, until golden. This is where a thermometer can be a great help, because the outside of a ham always looks 'done' very quickly but you want to make sure the middle of the ham is at least 80°C/175°F on a meat thermometer. Roast for a bit longer if it isn't up to temperature yet.

Remove from the oven, cover with foil again and allow the ham to sit for 10 minutes before carving.

To store any unused ham, wrap it in baking parchment and keep in the refrigerator. Clingfilm/plastic wrap or foil tend to make it a bit soggy. Also, we like to tear a bit off every time we walk by the fridge, so wrapping it in paper makes it easier to access! Eat within 1 week.

There's no doubt in my mind that roast ham joints on the bone are more succulent, tasty and tender, but suppliers do a fantastic job now of deboning ham joints, which makes them easier for the home cook.

SAUERKRAUT

Sauerkraut is a fine (and very easy) example of fermenting, and it's delicious with hot meat, like sausages, or spooned onto a mouthful of cured meat.

1 x green cabbage (I recommend Savoy Cabbage)

2 tablespoons sea salt

1 tablespoon caraway seeds

MAKES 1 JAR (ABOUT 200 G/7 OZ.)

Remove an outer leaf of the cabbage, rinse and set aside – don't worry if it tears a bit.

Chop the cabbage into thin slices, removing the stalk in the middle.

In a mixing bowl, sprinkle the salt and caraway seeds over the cabbage, and then massage with your hands for 5 minutes, squeezing the salt into the cabbage so that it reduces and starts to draw out the moisture. Set aside for at least 1 hour, until more water is drawn out and gathers at the bottom.

Sterilize a jar, and then put the cabbage and liquid in the jar. If you have more than about 4 or 5 tablespoonsful of liquid, drain a little bit away. (The liquid shouldn't come higher than the cabbage.)

Squash the cabbage down in the jar and then push the reserved leaf down on top, so that there is air above the leaf but no gap below it.

Store at room temperature for 3–4 days, then transfer to the refrigerator for 1 day before serving. Store in the refrigerator for up to 1 month.

HOME PICKLED CUCUMBER

1 pickling cucumber (e.g., ridge cucumber or gherkin)

3 tablespoons sea salt

200 ml/generous ¾ cup water

1 clove garlic, chopped

1 shallot, chopped

a pinch of freshly ground black pepper

2 bay leaves

a pinch of dried cinnamon

3 tablespoons distilled white vinegar

MAKES 1 JAR (ABOUT 200 G/7 OZ.)

The world of curing, preserving and fermenting is fascinating – from sushi to salt beef, it exists in almost every cuisine of the world. It's in the accompaniments too, like this recipe for curing cucumber or gherkins at home.

Slice the cucumber either crossways or lengthways and lay it on a plate. Sprinkle 1 tablespoon salt over the top and leave for 1 hour, to draw out a lot of the moisture.

Rinse the cucumber slices and pat dry with paper towels. Sterilize a jar, and then put the cucumber slices into the jar.

Put the water and remaining salt into a saucepan and bring to the boil to make a brine. Remove from the heat and let cool a little, so it's not boiling hot.

Add the garlic, shallot, pepper, bay leaves and cinnamon to the jar, and shake. Add the vinegar, then pour the brine over the top.

Seal the lid and leave in the refrigerator for 2–3 days, before serving. Store in the refrigerator for up to 1 month.

SIDE DISHES AND ACCOMPANIMENTS

ASPARAGUS AND PROSCIUTTO GRATIN

This is a delightful side dish to serve when asparagus is in season. It doesn't take much effort to put together and is always a crowd-pleaser at dinner parties.

12 **asparagus spears**

20 g/generous 1 tablespoon **butter**

150 ml/⅔ cup **crème fraîche/sour cream**

1 teaspoon freshly chopped **parsley**

6 slices **prosciutto**

2 teaspoons **breadcrumbs**

2 teaspoons finely grated **Parmesan cheese**

sea salt and freshly ground black pepper

roasting pan, greased

SERVES 2

Bend each asparagus spear until it snaps, and discard the woody ends. Steam the asparagus spears over a pan of boiling water for about 3–4 minutes, just to soften them – you don't want them fully cooked. Set aside.

Meanwhile, melt the butter in a frying pan/skillet and then stir in the crème fraîche/sour cream. Add the chopped parsley, season with salt and pepper, and remove from the heat.

Preheat the grill/broiler to medium.

Wrap a slice of prosciutto around 2 asparagus spears and lay them in the ovenproof roasting dish. Repeat with the remaining prosciutto slices and asparagus spears, laying them side by side in the dish.

Pour the melted butter and crème fraîche/sour cream mixture evenly over the top. Mix the breadcrumbs and Parmesan cheese together in a bowl and then sprinkle this over the top.

Grill/broil for 6–8 minutes, until nicely browned on top, then serve immediately.

'SWEET PATATAS BRAVAS'

Every time I go to a tapas restaurant with friends, we'll be going through the meat dishes and then someone will say, 'Ooooh, Patatas Bravas, yes?', which is met with a chorus of 'Patatas Bravas', 'Patatas Bravas' – so I think that people (or my friends and family, at least) enjoy saying 'Patatas Bravas' as much as they like eating it. So, here's a recipe for which I suggest using sweet potatoes, but you can use whichever type of potatoes you like.

FOR THE SAUCE

1 tablespoon olive oil

1 onion

1 garlic clove

1 teaspoon tomato purée/paste

2 teaspoons paprika

a pinch of dried chilli/hot pepper flakes

1 teaspoon soft/packed brown sugar

a big pinch of freshly chopped parsley, plus extra to garnish

a pinch of freshly chopped or dried basil

1 tablespoon red wine vinegar

400-g/714-oz. can of tomatoes, chopped

sea salt and freshly ground black pepper

FOR THE POTATOES

3 large sweet potatoes, cut roughly into cubes (I'm a big fan of keeping the peel on, but it's up to you)

2 tablespoons olive oil

SERVES 4

First, make the sauce. Ideally, make this the day before you want to serve it or follow the instructions to cool below.

Heat the olive oil in a frying pan/skillet over medium heat. Add the onion and fry it until soft and browning, then add the garlic and fry briefly. Add the tomato purée/paste, paprika, chilli/hot pepper flakes, sugar, parsley and basil, season with salt and pepper, and cook, stirring, for 1 minute. Add the vinegar and canned tomatoes, then reduce the heat and simmer for 5–6 minutes, until it thickens a little. Remove from the heat.

If you're making this the day before, let the mixture cool to room temperature, then place it in the refrigerator overnight (it will keep in an airtight container in the refrigerator for up to 3 days, or it can be frozen for another time). If you're making this sauce on the day you want to serve it, I strongly recommend cooling then reheating it before you pour it over the roasted potato pieces, because this really brings out the flavours. So, just fill a sink with cold water and lower the bottom of the pan into the water (or transfer the mixture to a bowl to lower into the water, to be even quicker) and keep stirring until the sauce is cool and thicker still. Set aside.

Preheat the oven to 180°C (350°F) Gas 4.

Put the potatoes in a pan, cover with cold water, bring to the boil and boil for 5 minutes to soften them. Drain well, then transfer them to a baking sheet and spread them out in a single layer. Drizzle the olive oil over the top and mix them around so they're well covered.

Roast in the preheated oven for 15–20 minutes and give them a shake halfway through. If you have peeled the potatoes they won't take as long to roast, so just reduce the cooking time a little.

While the potatoes are roasting, reheat the sauce by gently heating it in a saucepan on the hob/stovetop over low heat.

Remove the roasted potatoes from the oven and pop them into individual dishes to serve (or transfer to one large serving dish). Pour the reheated sauce over the potatoes. Serve immediately, garnished with extra parsley.

SWEET CHILLI STICKY SWEETCORN

A lovely accompaniment to serve with a main course/entrée or with a salumi platter.

1 whole corn cob, leaves and 'silk' stripped off

20 g/generous 1 tablespoon butter

½ fresh red chilli/chile, deseeded and finely chopped (or use a pinch of dried chilli/hot pepper flakes)

2 teaspoons white wine vinegar

3 tablespoons demerara/raw sugar

a squeeze of fresh lime juice

SERVES 4

Cook the corn cob in a pan of boiling water for 10 minutes over medium heat, until tender, then drain and cool slightly.

Melt the butter in a frying pan/skillet over medium heat and fry the chilli/chile on its own for 2 minutes. Add the vinegar, sugar and 2 tablespoons water, stir well and bring to the boil. Reduce the heat to a low simmer and cook until the mixture reduces and becomes sticky.

Meanwhile, using a sharp knife, carefully cut the corn kernels off the cob. Stir the corn kernels into the sticky mixture in the frying pan/skillet.

Remove from the heat and transfer the mixture to a dish. Leave to cool for at least 5 minutes before serving – be careful to let it cool sufficiently, because the sugar is caramelized and very hot.

This can also be served cold. Pop it into an airtight container and keep in the refrigerator for up to 3 days.

SALUMI CHIPS (BAKED SALUMI)

So simple and yet so moreish. I've tried this with lots of different varieties of salumi and, as you'll see in the Pasta Bake recipe in chapter 4 (see page 110), it's also a great addition to a main dish. This is a slightly leaner way to enjoy charcuterie too, as you'll see some of the fat drain out of it. I have to say that my personal favourite for this is saucisson sec, but feel free to try it with any slices of charcuterie, such as recipe-cured (salami, chorizo, etc, where the meat is minced/ground and mixed with flavourings) or straight-cured (prosciutto, for example, where whole joints of meat are cured).

12 slices salumi of your choice

MAKES 12

Preheat the oven to 180°C (350°F) Gas 4.

Lay the slices of salumi in a single layer on a baking sheet. Bake in the preheated oven for 20–25 minutes, until crisp. Keep checking that they're not burning. Remove from the oven and let cool.

Store in an airtight container in the refrigerator. These chips will last for up to a week in the refrigerator and are the perfect thing to nibble on.

CELERIAC REMOULADE

½ celeriac/celery root, peeled and grated

freshly squeezed juice of ½ lemon (see Cook's Note)

1 teaspoon mustard (Dijon/French or wholegrain are best)

a big pinch of freshly chopped parsley

a pinch of fennel seeds

a pinch of sea salt

SERVES 4

Combine all the ingredients in a bowl, mixing them together well, and chill in the refrigerator, covered, for at least 1 hour before serving so that the flavours can be absorbed.

Cook's Note
Add the freshly squeezed juice of ½ lemon first and then taste and add a little more, if you like.

APPLE SLAW

You'll see quite a lot of sour or acidic ingredients in the accompaniments and the recipes. They go so well with the rich, salty salumi, so it really reaches the far sides of your taste buds. Here's a slaw recipe with a sour apple taste.

1 tablespoon cider vinegar

2 tablespoons mayonnaise

¼ white cabbage, cored and shredded

1 carrot, grated

4–5 spring onions/scallions, finely chopped

a big pinch of freshly chopped parsley

2 eating/dessert apples, cored and coarsely grated (leave the peel on)

sea salt and freshly ground black pepper

SERVES 2–3

Pop all the ingredients into a bowl and mix well. Be sure to taste the slaw and then adjust the seasoning and add more of anything to suit your taste. Cover and refrigerate until you are ready to serve.

Try to make this at least 1 hour before serving, so that you can chill it really well and allow the flavours to mingle – this creates a delightful contrast with salumi.

FIG CHUTNEY

25 g/2 tablespoons butter

1 red onion, finely diced

12 fresh figs, peeled and chopped

40 g/1 ½ oz. soft/packed brown sugar

3 tablespoons red wine vinegar

a pinch of ground ginger

a handful of sultanas/golden raisins

freshly squeezed juice of ¼ lemon

MAKES 1 JAR (ABOUT 200G/ 7 OZ.)

Melt the butter in a frying pan/skillet, then add the onion and fry over a fairly high heat until it's soft and starting to brown. Stir in the figs and sugar, then add the vinegar, ginger and sultanas/golden raisins. Add the lemon juice and 3 tablespoons water. Reduce the heat to a low simmer and cook, uncovered, for 10–15 minutes, until the mixture thickens, stirring occasionally.

Remove from the heat and let cool, then transfer to a sterilized jar or a suitable airtight container and cover. Store in the refrigerator. It is best to make this chutney at least 24 hours before serving, to allow the flavours to mature.

Cook's Note

This chutney will keep (if sealed) for a couple of weeks in the refrigerator. You can also freeze it (in an airtight container). Just check the flavour after you defrost it, as it might need a little top-up of seasoning – perhaps a little more ground ginger or a squeeze of fresh lemon juice.

CARAMELIZED RED ONIONS

1 red onion, thinly sliced
2 tablespoons runny honey

SERVES 2

Preheat the oven to 180°C (350°F) Gas 4.

Put the onion in an ovenproof dish (see Cook's Note), drizzle over the honey and stir to mix so that the onions are well coated.

Roast in the preheated oven for about 15 minutes, until caramelized. Roast for longer if you want them chewy and crispy. If you're doing a bigger batch, it's worth giving them a shimmy around so that they all get a chance to caramelize.

You can freeze this in portions for 6 months, or it'll keep in the refrigerator in a sealed container for up to 2 weeks.

Cook's Note
These caramelized onions get very sticky, so I tend to line the ovenproof dish with foil, with the edges folded in, so that I can throw it away, rather than scrub sticky onions off the dish.

PUTTANESCA RELISH

This relish is quite like the Olive Tapenade (see below), but it's lighter and not as rich. It can be used to add to sandwiches and recipes, but it's also lovely served with a charcuterie board and spooned onto the meats.

50 g/2 oz. pitted black or Kalamata olives

2 canned anchovy fillets, drained

2 teaspoons capers, drained

a big pinch of freshly chopped coriander/cilantro

½ garlic clove

1 tablespoon olive oil

200-g/7-oz. can of tomatoes, drained (so you just have the pulp without too much liquid)

sea salt and freshly ground black pepper

MAKES 1 JAR (ABOUT 200 G/7 OZ.)

Pop all the ingredients into a food processor and whizz until the pieces are nice and small and the texture is relatively smooth. I still like a few small chunks, so I stop before it becomes more like a purée.

Transfer the mixture to a small, sterilized jar or an airtight container, or divide it between two ramekins and cover.

This relish will keep for a week or two in a sealed container in the refrigerator. It is also suitable for freezing. If you do freeze it, defrost it slowly in the refrigerator and then taste before you serve it, topping up any of the flavours that you think need a boost – perhaps the coriander/cilantro or the garlic.

Cook's Note
If you're eating this relish straightaway, you can mix in a little crème fraîche/sour cream to make it slightly creamy, if you like. This won't then keep beyond a day in the refrigerator though, so only mix it in just before you serve it.

OLIVE TAPENADE

This is a great mixture to have in a jar in the refrigerator to add to sandwiches.

50 g/2 oz. pitted black olives

2 canned anchovy fillets, drained

1 teaspoon capers, drained

1 tablespoon olive oil

a squeeze of fresh lemon juice

5 fresh basil leaves

1 teaspoon tomato purée/paste

sea salt and freshly ground black pepper

MAKES 1 JAR (ABOUT 200 G/7 OZ.)

Pop all the ingredients into a food processor and whizz until the pieces are nice and small and the texture is relatively smooth. I still like a few small chunks, so I stop before it becomes more like a purée.

Transfer the mixture to a small, sterilized jar or an airtight container, or divide it between two ramekins and cover.

This tapenade keeps for at least a week in a sealed container in the refrigerator. It is also suitable for freezing in portions. If you do freeze it, defrost it slowly in the refrigerator and taste before you serve it – you might like to add a little more basil or a squeeze more lemon juice.

CHUNKY BBQ SAUCE

I don't know about you, but a poor-quality BBQ sauce can ruin a great plate of meat for me. It's so easy to make it at home and I hope you taste the difference (and delight in it) when enjoying fresh BBQ sauce as quickly as I did.

50 g/3½ tablespoons butter

1 onion, chopped

2 teaspoons tomato purée/paste

2 tablespoons soft/packed brown sugar

1 teaspoon paprika

a pinch of chipotle powder

2 teaspoons Worcestershire sauce

1 teaspoon English/hot mustard powder

2 tablespoons white wine vinegar

a pinch each of sea salt and freshly ground black pepper

MAKES ABOUT
125 ML/½ CUP

Melt the butter in a frying pan/skillet over medium heat, then add the onion and fry until soft and browned. Add the tomato purée/paste, sugar, paprika and chipotle powder, and stir well. Add the Worcestershire sauce, mustard powder and vinegar, and season with salt and pepper, then as soon as it bubbles, pour in 150 ml/⅔ cup water. Increase the heat to high and bring to the boil, then let it boil hard, uncovered, for about 10 minutes, until the mixture reduces and thickens.

Remove from the heat and let cool, then whizz it in a food processor. I like to keep BBQ sauce nice and chunky, but you can keep whizzing until it's smooth, if you prefer.

SWEET AND FEISTY CRÈME FRAICHE

This is lovely served with the Cured Pork Kebab Skewers (see page 122) or the Slow-cooked, Dry-rub Pork Ribs with BBQ Sauce (see page 113), for example. It's got a bit of a kick but also a sweetness and freshness, so it's ideal to soften a rich serving of cured meat.

2 tablespoons crème fraîche/sour cream

1 teaspoon chipotle powder

4 pinches of cayenne pepper

2 teaspoons maple syrup

SERVES 4

Put all the ingredients into a bowl and stir to mix them together. Serve immediately or cover and keep refrigerated for up to 2 days.

HOMEMADE CHIPOTLE KETCHUP

This is lovely and light, and is perfect to serve with some of the heavier main course/ entrée dishes in Chapter 4. This recipe makes plenty for a large gathering.

20 g/generous 1 tablespoon butter

1 onion, chopped

1 cooking apple, peeled, cored and chopped

1 teaspoon chipotle powder

2 teaspoons paprika

1 teaspoon sea salt

100 ml/⅓ cup cider vinegar

3 x 400-g/7-oz. cans of chopped tomatoes

100 g/scant ½ cup soft/packed brown sugar

MAKES ABOUT
500 G/1¼ LBS.

Melt the butter in a saucepan over medium heat and fry the onion until soft. Add the apple and continue to cook, stirring, for another minute or two. Add the chipotle powder, paprika and salt, then stir in the vinegar and bring to the boil.

Drain off about half of the juice from the cans of tomatoes – you don't need that much juice – then add the rest of the canned tomatoes and juice to the pan. Bring to the boil, then reduce the heat and simmer for 45 minutes, stirring occasionally.

Stir in the sugar and leave to simmer for a further 45 minutes, stirring occasionally.

Remove from the heat and let cool, then whizz the mixture in a food processor. You can leave it a little chunky if you like, or keep whizzing until it's smooth. Decant the ketchup into sterilized bottles or containers and seal or cover. Keep refrigerated for up to 3 weeks, or you can freeze it, if you like.

WARM INFUSED OLIVES

These olives are perfect to serve with any cured meats. Make sure you put some crusty bread with them too, so that guests can soak up the delicious oil.

3 tablespoons olive oil

1 garlic clove, finely chopped

¼ fresh red chilli/chile, deseeded and finely chopped

a pinch of ground ginger

a good squeeze of fresh lime juice

150–200 g/5–7 oz. unseasoned green or black olives

sea salt and freshly ground black pepper

SERVES 2

Start with about one-third of the olive oil in a frying pan/skillet, heat it over medium heat, then add the garlic, chilli/chile, ginger and lime juice, and fry until the garlic and chilli/chile pieces are brown and crispy. Add the rest of the olive oil and continue to fry until bubbling.

Reduce the heat right down to a simmer and throw in the olives. Stir for a few minutes to heat them through, making sure that the olives don't cook on the bottom of the frying pan/skillet.

Remove from the heat, add salt and pepper to taste, then transfer the mixture to a heatproof dish. Serve.

This mixture will keep in the refrigerator for up to 5 days; you might just have to warm it through again before serving to melt any oil that has set.

WHOLEMEAL CRISPBREAD

The crispbread is a lovely thing to have with charcuterie, particularly the pâtés and rillettes, which are wonderfully rich.

1 tablespoon sunflower oil

100 g/generous ¾ cup wholemeal/whole-wheat flour

1 tablespoon water

a pinch of baking powder

a pinch of salt

a large baking sheet, greased

MAKES 8

Pre-heat the oven to 180°C (350°F) Gas 4.

Mix all the ingredients really well in a bowl, and add a touch more water if it feels really dry. Bring it together into a dough.

Place the dough onto a flour-dusted surface and roll it into a large, thin circle or rectangle, certainly no more than 5 mm/¼ inch thick.

Transfer the rolled dough to the prepared baking sheet, using the rolling pin to help you lift it. Score the surface into slices with a knife (like pizza slices or little rectangles). Try and go quite deep with this, and don't worry if you nick all the way through the crispbread.

Bake in the preheated oven for 20–25 minutes, until crisp.

Remove from the oven and let cool until it is cool enough to touch, then carefully break it along the scored lines. The sooner you can do this the better, so don't let it go completely cold before you do it.

HOME-BAKED OATCAKES

Yum, I love oatcakes. I would choose them over any other savoury biscuit/cracker in all the world, even if that decision was forever. I'm serious. Try me.

100 g/3¾ oz. rolled/porridge oats

50 g/scant ½ cup plain/all-purpose flour

40 g/3 tablespoons butter (at room temperature)

a pinch of baking powder

a pinch of sea salt

additions as you wish – see Cook's Note (optional)

milk, for brushing

4-cm/1½-inch round or square cookie cutter
a large baking sheet, greased

MAKES ABOUT 14

Preheat the oven to 180°C (350°F) Gas 4.

Put everything (except the milk for brushing) into a bowl and mix really well with your hands, crumbling the ingredients together. Add 2 tablespoons cold water, a little at a time, mixing with your hands, until you have a soft dough.

Place the dough onto a flour-dusted surface and roll it out to the thickness that you'd like. Use the cookie cutter (or the top of a glass) to stamp out circles or squares and then pop them on the prepared baking sheet, leaving a little space between each one. Brush a little milk over the top of each one.

Bake in the preheated oven on the middle shelf for 12–15 minutes. Transfer to a wire rack and let cool completely. Store in an airtight container for a week or two. You can freeze them for up to 6 months.

Cook's Note

You can mix all sorts of things into your oatcakes. Some of the classic ones are herbs, dried fruit pieces, crushed roast (peeled) chestnuts, finely grated lime or lemon zest, or dried chilli/hot pepper flakes.

CROSTINO

Another traditional Italian bread accompaniment made using ciabatta.

1 ciabatta loaf, thinly sliced
olive oil, to drizzle
sea salt and freshly ground black pepper

SERVES 4

Preheat the grill/broiler to medium.

Cut the ciabatta loaf into 1 cm/½ inch slices.

Drizzle some olive oil onto a large baking sheet and then lay the ciabatta slices on top. Drizzle a little more olive oil over the top of the slices, then sprinkle with salt and pepper. Grill/broil the slices for 4–5 minutes, turning halfway through. Serve immediately.

GARLIC-Y BRUSCHETTA

This is such an easy accompaniment for so many of the recipes in Chapters 2 and 3.

1 baguette
1 garlic clove, peeled
olive oil, to drizzle

SERVES 4

Preheat the grill/broiler to medium.

Slice the baguette diagonally into 1 cm/½ inch slices. Rub the garlic clove around the edge of the baguette slices – the hard crust will rub the flavour off the garlic clove without overpowering the bread.

Drizzle olive oil onto a baking sheet and then lay the baguette slices on top. Drizzle a little more olive oil over the top of the slices. Grill/broil for 4–5 minutes, turning halfway through. Serve immediately.

MELBA TOAST

2 slices white or wholemeal/
whole-wheat bread

sea salt and freshly ground black
pepper

MAKES 16 PIECES

Preheat the grill/broiler to medium.

Cut the top crust off each slice of bread. Lightly toast the bread on both sides, either under the preheated grill/broiler or using a toaster on a low setting.

Remove from the grill/broiler or toaster and slice horizontally through the middle of each slice of toast to halve the thickness, then cut each slice diagonally both ways to make 4 triangles. You should now have 16 triangles.

Lay the triangles on a baking sheet with the untoasted sides facing up, sprinkle salt and pepper over the top and then pop them under the preheated grill/broiler for 1–2 minutes, until the tops are toasted. Serve immediately.

INDEX

ACKNOWLEDGEMENTS

Thank you to Julia, Kate, Lauren and everyone at the publishers of this book. You are so kind and positive and I am so lucky to get to work for you on another book. To Heather for helping it be possible. And to the incredible photographer, Steve, for turning my scribbles and mobile phone photos into something that looks this good.

To Trealy Farm, Guild of Fine Foods, Great Glen Game and all the places where I got to learn more about the wonderful scope of cured meats.

To Jon, Mike and Sandy, for being literally on board, you are so important to us. And there's a guy called Nick. I won't go into it, but basically he's why this incredible Muddy Boots journey is still going.

John, Sarah, Dunc, Alex, Dan and Linda – the most graceful, generous, loving family at the source of all things Muddy Boots.

My wonderful sister, who has helped me all my life. My father, whom I admire most in all the world. And my gorgeous mother, who taught me the simplest, everlasting rule of a kitchen: that it is a place to play and have fun and just enjoy whatever you're trying.

And finally Ro. Nothing I write even comes close ... I'll find the words one day.